HOW TO DECLUTTER YOUR MIND

Secrets to Stop Overthinking, Relieve Anxiety, and Achieve Calmness and Inner Peace, and Eliminate Negative Thinking, Decluttering Your Home

Michelle Coty joseph bartkowiak

© Copyright 2020 by Michelle Coty joseph bartkowiak

All rights reserved.

This document is geared towards providing exact and reliable information regarding the topic and issue covered. The publication is sold with the idea that the publisher is not required to render accounting, officially permitted, or otherwise qualified services. If advice is necessary, legal or professional, a practiced individual in the profession should be ordered.

From a Declaration of Principles which was accepted and approved equally by a Committee of the American Bar Association and a Committee of Publishers and Associations.

In no way is it legal to reproduce, duplicate, or transmit any part of this document in either electronic means or printed format. Recording of this publication is strictly prohibited, and any storage of this document is not allowed unless with written permission from the publisher. All rights reserved.

The information provided herein is stated to be truthful and consistent, in that any liability, in terms of inattention or otherwise, by any usage or abuse of any policies, processes, or directions contained within is the solitary and utter responsibility of the recipient reader. Under no circumstances will any legal responsibility or blame be held against the publisher for any reparation, damages, or monetary loss due to the information herein, either directly or indirectly.

Respective authors own all copyrights not held by the publisher.

The information herein is offered for informational purposes solely and is universal as so. The presentation of the information is without a contract or any type of guarantee assurance.

The trademarks that are used are without any consent, and the publication of the trademark is without permission or backing by the trademark owner. All trademarks and brands within this book are for clarifying purposes only and are owned by the owners themselves, not affiliated with this document.

TABLE OF CONTENTS

Introduction 1

Chapter 1: What Is Mental Clutter? 9

  Mental clutter is not a disease, but it is also nothing less than that 9

    Before we move any further, let us go through the story of Mary 10

  The Human Brain- Fascinating But Inefficient Storage Device 15

  What is the Mental Clutter? 18

  Decluttering of the Mind 20

Chapter 2: Mental Clutter- An Infinite Loop of Thoughts That Keep Us Trapped 22

  Life is Not Meant to Be Pointless 25

  Thoughts- Your Creation.. 26

Chapter 3: Why Our Brains Become Cluttered? 30

  Stress 32

    We Do Not Have a Reason to be Stressed 32

    Despite All This, the Stress is a Stark Reality 33

    Stress Can Have Physical Implications 37

  Hoarding of Thoughts and Memories 51

  Negative Thought Patterns.. 55

    Carelessness Could Have Got Us Killed 55

    Negative Thought Patterns Kept Us Alert 56

    Numbing fear all the time is irrational 57

    Indecision, Irrationality, Fright, and Weakness....58
    Repetition of The Same Thoughts Over And
    Over Again...58
    You will Have To Become Conscious Of The
    Negative Thought Patterns 58

Chapter 4: The 8 Common Symptoms of Clutter 60

Chapter 5: Why Mental Clutter is Even More Dangerous Than We Think? 72

    Five Main Areas Affected by Mental Clutter: 74

Chapter 6: Can We Stop the Constant Chatter of Thoughts in the Mind? 83

    Peace of Mind is an Incorrect Objective 83
    Thoughtlessness is Impossible 84
    Bring Clarity Between the Conscious and the
    Subconscious Mind 85
    You will Need to Be Systematic 88
    Carefully Choose What You Ingest 93
    Use Your Mind Consciously 99

Chapter 7: What Does Decluttering the Thoughts Mean? 104

    Meditation- The Path to Detachment from the
    Mental Clutter 106
    Guided Meditation Practice For Bringing Awareness
    of Thoughts 110

Chapter 8: What Are You Missing While Working With A Cluttered Mind? 123

Chapter 9: Is Decluttering Really Effective and Possible? 130

  Important Parts of the Decluttering Process 132

Chapter 10: The Efficiency of Decluttering Depends on 3 Important Things 141

  Process 142

  Practice 145

  Purpose 148

Chapter 11: Effective Ways to Declutter Your Mind. 152

  Deep Breathing 153

  Meditation 163

    The Way to Untangle Your Thoughts 163

  Guided Meditation 174

  Mindfulness 192

    Living in the Mind 194

    Living in the Present 195

    Path to Become Mindful 199

    Awareness of Thoughts 205

    Let Go of Negative Thoughts and Emotions 211

Chapter 12: Decluttering Your Life and Responsibilities 212

  Lay Focus on Your Core Values to Avoid Deviation and Dilemma 216

  Become More Objective and Bring Clarity of Vision 216

  Set Goals Mindfully 217

Understanding the Troubles With Multitasking 218
Paying Attention to Your Routines 220

Chapter 13: Decluttering Your Personal Life and Relationships 221

Learn to Look Beyond Possessions 222
Become Thrifty With Time 223
Create Space in Life 224
The Myth of Popularity 225
Dealing with Toxic Relationships 226

- The Reasons for Toxicity in Relationships 226
- It May Only Be Your Perception 227
- Inclusiveness 228
- Listen 229
- Speak Mindfully 229
- Let Other's Be 230
- Uncertainty 231
- Insecurities 231
- Hegemony 232
- Poor Boundaries 232
- Abusiveness 233
- Lack of Integrity 233
- Compatibility Issues 233
- The Options You Have 234
- Life Without That Person 234
- The Agony of Separation 234
- Do Not Involve Passion 235
- Handling negative Reaction 235

Chapter 14: Decluttering Your Home 237
   Make Living Space Livable 238
   Popular Decluttering Methods 239
   Preventing Future Clutter 247

Chapter 15: Decluttering Your Workspace 249
   Decluttering Your Desk 250
   Dealing with Clutter from Bosses and Coworkers 252

Chapter 16: Decluttering Your Time Spent Online ... 254
   Social Media Platforms Cluttering the Mind 255
      Declutter Your Feeds 257
      Limit Your Exposure Time 258
   Declutter Your Posts 258
      Ask the Question 'Why' 258
      Limit Your Posts 259

Conclusion 260

Introduction

Clutter is undesirable. It makes life difficult. Some people may take pride in the fact that they feel more at home with their clutter, but deep within, they know that dealing with clutter is never easy. It is comparatively easy to deal with physical clutter as you can easily dispose of all the things you do not need. However, that may not be the same with mental clutter.

Mental clutter can lead to:

Decision Fatigue: You may struggle with even insignificant decisions in your life.

- Do you become confused even in choosing the clothes for the day?
- Does ordering from the menu take longer than it should?
- Do you find yourself struggling with the thought of talking to someone specific but can never decide?

All these are signs of mental clutter.

Information Overload: You know too many things but do not know what to do with that information.

- Do you feel that you know much more than others, but when it comes to putting that information at work, you find yourself staring at a wall?
- Are you always trying to think too many things at the same time?
- Do you feel too much distracted when trying to figure out something that needs focus and attention?

Information overload is another major problem created by mental clutter because we start treating our mind as an unlimited capacity warehouse but have no system to sort that information. We pay no attention to classification and prioritization.

Mental Rut: You begin to feel the pointlessness of things in life. The only problem being that the life is not pointless, only you seemed to have lost your purpose and motivation. You feel the stagnation in life.

- Are you resisting change?
- Every day, do you feel that life is not taking you anywhere?
- Do you look forward to something with great anticipation and child-like enthusiasm?
- Have days of the week or the month started losing their significance for you?
- Do you feel that you lack the enthusiasm for everything in life?

Many people would easily term this state as depression, but it isn't. The mental rut is a chronic state in which your mind is becoming indifferent to various rewards the life has to offer.

When your mind is cluttered, it can blur the colors that make life vibrant and joyful.

Voices in the Head: We all have too much rumbling inside our heads while trying to accomplish something else. The thoughts may only look like mere distractions, but they are much more than that.

- Do you feel there is too much going inside your head all the time?
- Do you think that your mind is always driving you somewhere else?
- Do you keep getting reminded of past traumatic events?
- Are you unable to think, sleep, or be at peace?

People easily associate hearing voices in the head as mental illnesses, like schizophrenia or bipolar disorder. The fact is that we spend a quarter of our waking hours listening to our inner voices. You can call them gut feelings, instincts, flashes of the past events just before you attempt something similar, and the memories buried in the subconscious mind.

Therefore, all voices in the head do not mean that you are hallucinating. However, that doesn't even mean that all such voices are harmless. Voices in the head can be distracting, discouraging, and demotivating. They can lead to severe mood-swings in most people and may make accomplishing anything difficult. Mental clutter is largely responsible for such voices in the head. When you have too many unprocessed thoughts in your mind, they begin to process themselves on their own and cause trouble.

Monkey Mind: Buddhists call a mind with unsettled, restless, confused, uncontrollable, or fanciful ideas as a monkey mind.

- Do you think you don't have active control over the kind of thoughts your mind has?
- Do you keep dreaming of the future that never materializes?
- Do you feel indecisive most of the time?
- Do you think there are always too many unsettled thoughts floating in your mind?

Many people feel the unending mind chatter but cannot find a way to stop it. This mind chatter can make them restless and tired. It takes away all the peace and tranquillity in life. It can make accomplishing any goal difficult as doubt and indecision will become a consistent feature of life. The monkey mind is not a rare phenomenon but a common one. Most of the people in the world are suffering from it. Again, mental clutter is the culprit behind the monkey mind. If you want to tame the monkey mind, you must first learn to deal with the mental clutter.

This book is all about decluttering the mind and dealing with all the issues that arise with it. It will help you understand the cause of the mental clutter and help you declutter it with order and ease.

Congratulations on purchasing this book, and thank you for doing so.

Stress, doubt, negative thought patterns, and an excess of all the things we dread have become a regular feature of our lives. No matter how vehemently we may deny, we all have these in our lives, but most of us don't know their causes, and that's why the solution is always difficult.

This book will help you in understanding the real cause of mental clutter leading to distress. It will help you understand the cause and give you the tools to diagnose the symptoms.

Unending mind chatter can become painful and obstructing. When the mind is singing its song all the time, thinking anything productive can become difficult. It is not only disturbing but can also be dangerous in many ways. Most creators struggle with the issue but find no way to overcome it.

However, putting an end to the mind chatter is not an option that you have. You must know it from the beginning that there is no way you can stop your mind from having random thoughts. It is a skill it has developed over millions of years of evolution, and it is not going to give it up. Your problem is not the mind chatter but the way you are trying to deal with it.

This book will help you understand how to deal with mental chatter and how to remain unaffected.

This book will also explore mental clutter in detail and explain the visible and latent impact on life. It will also explain how it affects your health, relationships, career, and finances.

Decluttering of the mind is a crucial and unavoidable task. You can delay it as much as you like, but you must know that you will always be at the losing end.

A person with a decluttered mind can enjoy freedom from stress and anxiety. Such a person will have clarity of thought and continued growth. Living in the moment will become a reality for such a person. There will be no reason to remain plagued by the fears of the past and the future. Procrastination will come to an end in life, and things will get done.

Do you want to become such a person?

This book is a doorway to complete relaxation. It will explain the ways to declutter the mind and relax completely. It will also explain various relaxation techniques.

This book will help you with decluttering your life and responsibilities. You will be able to prioritize things in life and not run after random things. It will help you become more objective and goal-oriented. You will also learn the demerits of useless multi-tasking habits that we have picked and ways to shun such habits.

It will also help you in dealing with your personal life and relationships. You will learn ways to create more space in life for your loved ones. At the same time, this book will also teach you ways to deal with toxic relationships and prevent them from impacting you.

Decluttering your home and workspace is also equally important as it can also lead to mental clutter. The clutter in your home will keep your mind occupied and affect the way you live and think.

Clutter in the workplace can be physical as well as mental. The way you keep your desk, as well as your relationship with your coworkers and boss, will determine the way you think. Decluttering the home and the workplace is important for allowing the mind to think freely.

Last but not least is decluttering your digital life. We live in the age of the internet. Our social lives have shrunk a lot to the illuminated screens we possess. These screens have become the source of joys and sorrows in our lives, and most of us have begun losing our grip around reality. There was a time when people felt sad or happy due to real events. These days, a few likes- dislikes, and comments can become a matter of life or death for some people and may push many on the dark roads of sorrow.

This lack of control over our personal lives is our own doing. Our power of discernment of real and unreal gets weaker as we accumulate too much clutter in our minds. The more we increase our reliance on the digital platforms, the greater the amount of clutter we accumulate. We begin suffering from the malice of information overload but have no use for the information we accumulate.

This book will help you understand the main problems caused by reckless social media exposure and help you limit your social media presence to a reasonable level.

This book has been written in a straightforward and easy to understand way so that everyone can take advantage of this information.

You'll find that every section in the chapter has an equal focus on understanding the cause and resolving it. The steps will be easy and systematic so that you face no problem in implementing them.

I hope that you will be able to take full advantage of this book.

There are plenty of books on this subject on the market; thanks again for choosing this one!

Every effort has been made to ensure it is full of as much useful information as possible; please enjoy it!

Chapter 1: What Is Mental Clutter?

Mental clutter is not a disease, but it is also nothing less than that

It is a disability to be not able to feel the real joys and sorrows of life. It limits your ability to live a life free of stress and anxieties. It keeps you traumatized by the fears of the past and agonized by the dangers of the future.

Mental clutter works like a curse. It fills your mind with prejudice, and you begin to judge things all the time. It infects the mind with the disease of assuming things rather than trying to know or experience the truth, first hand.

Before we move any further, let us go through the story of Mary

One day Mary came back from the office. She had a long, tiring, and rough day. There was nothing in the day she liked. It was an uneventful and forgettable day like all the other days.

She'd hit the bed in a few hours and then would have to wake up the next morning again to another uneventful day.

She had her supper and was about to go to bed when she realized that she had an early morning appointment with her gynecologist. She couldn't miss the appointment as she had already waited very long for it.

But, she couldn't even take leave without informing her office as that was strictly against the official policy. Looking at the current job scenario, that would be an unnecessary risk to take. She pondered over the dreadful results of losing a job at the moment. She felt a chill going down her spine.

However, the fact remained that she needed to go to the doctor. She couldn't keep ignoring her health. There was no one else to look after her.

Now, she had to take the leave without going to the office.

The first thought was to email the boss about her appointment or send a text to her instead. However, what if the boss outrightly rejects her leave. She wasn't even very cordial with her in the evening. Maybe she was unhappy with the presentation she gave, or someone had been spreading rumors about her to the boss.

However, Mary was unable to pinpoint any problem with the presentation she gave. She had paid attention to every detail. But Mary knew that her boss was finicky. She never approved of anything.

Mary had worked so hard for the presentation and spent so many hours working on it. Yet, her boss didn't show the courtesy to say even a few words of appreciation. By this time, Mary's anger had started to build up. Every probable act of disregard shown by her boss started to flash in front of her eyes.

She remembered the events when she had accepted to work extra on her boss's single request, and that ungrateful lady was not ready to grant her a short leave of a few hours she needed for her important health check-up. She felt exasperated.

The more she thought of her boss, the angrier she got.

Her short leave was still hanging in the air. She needed that leave desperately.

She tried to push aside the idea of asking for leave from her boss directly because now she thought she knew that her boss didn't like her. There was no room for doubt.

She thought that she could ask her friend and coworker Becky to tell the boss about her absence. It looked a good idea but only for a moment.

She remembered that Becky was not particularly chatty with her today. She felt cold and distant. Mary couldn't even recall anything that might have made Becky feel so.

She tried to think of any event in the past that might have led to this indifference. She also recalled that Becky had even refused to go for a coffee the other day. Did that mean that even Becky had something in her mind against her? Was she plotting anything against her?

She could now recollect the times Becky had been with Rayan from the accounts who didn't think of her very highly.

Mary was getting at her wits' end. She couldn't think of a single person in that office whom she could trust. Mary felt as if everyone was conspiring against her. She had spent many years of her prime in that place, yet she didn't have one person to look up to. She felt antagonized.

She looked up the watch and realized that she had spent the better part of the night pondering over it. She had only a few hours to sleep and then had a very busy day ahead. But sleep was a difficult customer at that agitated state of mind. She didn't want to think about it anymore but could think about anything else.

The more she thought about it, the worse she felt about herself. She had failed to get friends or succeed in her life. Her anger started to turn into self-pity and remorse.

She wanted to sleep but was more worried that she wouldn't get up early in the morning and reach her office on time or make it to the doctor's office for her appointment.

Somehow Mary was able to sleep, and when she woke up, she was already late. She was angrier than she used to be.

She got ready and headed straight to her office.

She stormed the office of her boss and began shouting. Mary's boss wasn't even able to understand the matter.

Mary came, shouted, and resigned.

She had no intention of working with people who were indifferent, inconsiderate, and ungrateful.

The night before, she was worried about the prospect of being jobless, and the next morning she was jobless indeed. Yet, she was just angry and convinced of the things that were a product of her mind. She believed in the thoughts her mind produced and took them as the gospel truth.

Mental clutter can do a lot more damage than this to you.

It can be dangerous when you give your mind a free hand to have thoughts. Whenever it can, it will assume things and draw conclusions that suit it. It will go on a rampage and destroy something or the other.

All the dreams, hopes, failures, resentments, grudges, sufferings, stress, and anxieties you hold in your mind form mental clutter and obstruct the logical flow of thoughts. Whenever you are in a stressful situation or feel cornered, these thoughts get scrambled and begin loading themselves as destructive ammunition.

Have you ever noticed that when you are in a stressful situation, all of a sudden, you begin to have all the negative thoughts at once? Do you think it is just a coincidence?

It doesn't happen by chance. The survival mechanism in your brain kicks in. It begins to bring all the negative thoughts to mind to make you virtually the worst-case scenario so that you become fearful and avoid facing the real threat. That is the fight or flight response kicking in. It can make you take some of the worst decisions of life. The more clutter you have in your mind, the worse the scenarios would be.

It is the main reason most people begin to believe that their thoughts are their enemies. They feel that the constant bombarding of thoughts in their mind causes restlessness. They want to achieve a state of thoughtlessness—a state in which they can do away with their thoughts and experience complete calm.

Sadly, you cannot achieve that state. Our mind has around 50,000 thoughts a day. It is busy every moment of your life. It is always active.

It has practically unlimited capacity to have thoughts and store them. If you think that storing the thoughts is a problem and you are suffering from the lack of storage space, you are wrong.

The Human Brain- Fascinating But Inefficient Storage Device

Fascinating Storage Space

The storage space in our mind is vast. As per an article published in the Scientific American in 2010 and another Stanford study, the human brain's storage capacity is astonishing. It can store 2.5 petabytes of digital memory. It is around 2.5 million gigabytes of space. In simple words, you can record 300 years of a TV program or programs that could run for 2,628,000 hours in this much memory.

So anyone out there worrying about the mental capacity to record things need not worry. There is more than enough space to record anything that you may like.

However, knowingly or unknowingly, our race has taken that a tad bit too seriously, and we have made it an expedition to fill up our mind with all the trash that we can lay our hands-on.

We keep on absorbing as much information, thoughts, feelings, emotions as we can and never think of sorting it out, and this is where the problem begins.

Inefficient Retrieval Process

Although our brain has a fascinating storage capacity, it cannot retrieve the same with equal efficiency as it stores. Your subconscious works like a photocopier machine and records everything that it sees. However, when it comes to recalling that information as needed, the mind works like an unsystematic barn where you put haystack. Everything is the same, and there is no way you can identify minor details of most things.

Therefore, while your brain can store a lot, it can recall only a very insignificant amount of that information.

Now, the most important question is, **'what does the mind do with the rest of the information?'**

It is a million-dollar question because it has the answer to most of our mental problems.

A very big part of the information is in a fluid state floating in mind as thoughts, memories, and visuals. You keep getting them all the time, whether you want them or not.

Most of the time, the random thoughts you get are fairly recent. Fresh thoughts are more fluid in your memory. It is the reason you generally have dreams of recent events heavy on your mind. However, the mind can quickly pull out thoughts of related or unrelated events in panic or agitated state of mind. It is the reason you also get all sorts of fearful thoughts when you are frightened, agitated, or panicked.

We have the gift of this fascinating brain that can store a large amount of information and process thoughts quickly. However, when there is a frantic activity in the brain, the sorting process doesn't work well. You have many thoughts but may not have the required information needed at that point.

Do you remember cramming up information just before a crucial exam or have seen others doing the same?

It is not an unusual sight outside exam centers or outside interview rooms. People are trying to stuff too much information rapidly to get the required information when needed. However, most people would vouch that they were staring at a blank when they needed that information. They couldn't remember the fact they had crammed just a few minutes ago. The same people would also testify that they could remember all of it when they were not feeling stressed.

You can't push your brain to remember or forget something. You can train it a little, but that also has its limits.

Our problem is not about storing enough thoughts but of properly indexing, stacking, and retrieving the thoughts when we need them. The bigger problem is managing the negative thoughts floating in our minds, leading to self-destructive thinking.

What is the Mental Clutter?

Mental clutter is the accumulation of all the regrets that you've had in your life. It is the feeling of exasperation you experience at the back of your mind on missing all the opportunities in life. The mind keeps them fresh to keep you on edge.

The mind doesn't want you to rest. It wants you to be at the top of the game always, and that's the reason it never allows you to forget your failures.

All the things that you should have done but remain unfinished float in your mind as clutter. Although they are not fulfilling their purpose, the mind would never allow you to forget that you missed on accomplishing them. They would also play their part in inciting fear and regret when the time comes.

All the unfinished business you've kept on long standby past the due date will also float as mental clutter.

All your worries, fears, and insecurities also add to the clutter. They lead to the generation of negative thought patterns in which all the other things would act as fuel.

Your resentments, grudges against others, criticism, longings, unfulfilled dreams, and fears of failures also play the role of active ingredients.

All these things act as the top layer of lava that's hot, fluid, and fiery. The memories buried deep within your subconscious mind acts as the solid core that would keep providing such thoughts the heat of fear and procrastination.

Mental clutter has the power to keep you in a state of a mental rut. You'll keep feeling stagnated, stuck, aimless, hopeless, and a little desperate with no way in view to break the shackles.

If you have mental clutter, you'll begin doubting most of your decisions and struggle endlessly with the problem of choice. Making quick and firm decisions will become difficult. It has nothing to do with your skill, knowledge, or expertise but due to poor discernment. You fail to distinguish between right and wrong.

You'd know that you are struggling with the information you hold in your mind, and yet you'd seek more and more information in desperation to get better clarity and knowledge.

Mental clutter begins an endless cycle. You feel trapped as if stuck in quicksand. You know that humping, wriggling, and struggling in desperation will get you stuck deeper, yet you invariably do all that in desperation.

Decluttering of the Mind

The decluttering of the mind is the simple process of understanding the clutter in mind and then systematically dealing with it. By now, you may have understood that your mind will never struggle with a lack of space. There is just too much of space in mind. But, it certainly doesn't have the power to retrieve all that data stored in the mind when needed.

Decluttering the mind helps you in reducing the load of incoming information. It makes you understand that you do not need to know everything. You do not need to know things that do not concern you. You do not need to memorize things only to impress others. You do not need to hoard information in your mind, which is easily available on the internet.

Most importantly, you do not need to retain your fears, anxieties, regrets, and grudges that only create problems for you. It helps you in obstructing such inflow and also properly offloading some of the information you already possess. Getting rid of the baggage of the past is an important exercise in decluttering the mind.

If you want to live your life fully without fears and anxieties, then decluttering the mind is the way.

The mental chatter that causes the highest amount of discomfort is not the real problem. Most people waste a large amount of their time in pursuit of quieting the mind. It is a futile pursuit. There is no way you can quieten the mind until you die. Detachment and distancing is the correct way to take.

We are highly identified with the thoughts we have. We live in the delusion that we and our thoughts are the same. It is a misconception. Our thoughts are just a small part of our being and not the whole of our existence. There are ways you can learn to distance yourself from your thoughts, and the mental chatter would stop causing so much nuisance in your life. Learning to distance yourself from your thoughts and becoming an observer is an important part of decluttering the mind.

Let me warn you in the beginning that there are no shortcuts for decluttering of the mind. There is no way you will be able to trick your mind. The mind is where all the tricks originate.

Decluttering the mind is a long process that would take a lot of practice and discipline. You would need to change the way you think and break several thought patterns in the process. However, it is a doable task.

With some practice and perseverance, you will be able to declutter your mind and gain the freedom to live your life free of all the stress, anxiety, and fears that plague you at the moment.

Chapter 2: Mental Clutter- An Infinite Loop of Thoughts That Keep Us Trapped

Most of the time, Greek mythology looks a bit over the top or extreme. Looking at Gods indulging in petty acts and useless conflicts, you may not have a great view about them. Nevertheless, Greek stories have a deep meaning about the futility of life, human nature, and vices. While dealing with deeper meanings of life, these stories also make us understand that not even the gods are infallible.

One such is the story of the King of Corinth called Sisyphus. He was a clever ruler and was famous for playing tricks, even on the Gods. He cheated death twice in his lifetime and was so infamous that even Thanatos or the personification of death was afraid to go near him.

However, even Sisyphus was unable to evade death forever and eventually died in the ripe old age. He knew it very well that when he reaches the underworld after his death, the gods will unleash their wrath on his soul, but that was destiny.

In Greek mythology, the Gods have been shown to punish people in very cruel ways. But the punishment that was given to Sisyphone was not cruel by its means. It was a punishment that personified the futility of life.

When Sisyphus died, Zeus, the great God, didn't give him the 'famed' cruel tortures. What Sisyphus bore as a punishment is what we call the circle of life.

Sisyphus was given the task of carrying a large boulder up a steep hill. It was a tiresome task but nothing that Sisyphus couldn't accomplish. The only problem was that as he was about to reach the top, the boulder would somehow slide back, and Sisyphus would have to begin the journey all over again.

The simple task of taking a boulder up the hill became a punishment only because it was a repetitive and monotonous task. Sisyphus was cursed to remain trapped. He had to follow a routine he couldn't break. He had to suffer the monotonous nature of life. He was a person who played pranks even on Gods in his lifetime and had an eventful life. Now, he had a life in front of him that offered no respite from the same thing. There was no change in view, and that was punishment enough in itself.

If you self-introspect, you'll find that most of us are suffering from this Sisyphus syndrome. We are living an automated life, achieving automated goals, and have automated aspirations.

If you stress your brain, you'd be able to pinpoint a very few people, if at all, who are not living automated lives. It is the reason most of us are suffering and begin to find life pointless beyond a point.

The pointlessness of life and its sufferings are not visible until you are struggling with fulfilling your necessities. Till that point, your mind remains focused on survival. You are more worried about the next meal or shelter. However, as soon as you come above the survival struggles, you begin to feel the pointlessness of life. Beyond a point, there is nothing to achieve. Your failures of the past, struggles, desperations, and your despondencies begin to take effect on your mind.

You suffer not only your failures but also your successes. Satisfaction, peace, and calm are always far away. Your mind is always occupied with one or the other desperation and keeps making life difficult.

Life is Not Meant to Be Pointless

A big myth that begins to develop in our minds is about the pointlessness of life. As we move ahead, fail, succeed, fail again, keep failing, or keep succeeding, we begin losing the perspective of life.

Life is never pointless. Life has a purpose. Its purpose is to achieve a higher state of consciousness.

However, we are so immersed in the personal melodrama of life that we begin to think that the chaos around us is life.

The incorrect perception is a result of mental clutter. When we emphasize insignificant things in life, our mind begins treating them as important, and this clutter gets the top space in the fluid thoughts.

Insignificant details around us, something said by someone about us, an eye contact avoided by someone, and several other such things that don't even mean anything get a prominent space in our thought process.

Your mind is always actively thinking, processing, assuming, and deciphering such things and creating more clutter that's mostly baseless.

However, as you know, it takes a lot of effort to keep things tidy, and you only need to leave things idle for cobwebs to come up and dust to settle on the surface.

When you allow your mind to work without productive or positive thoughts, stress, doubt, indecision, and negative bias is easy to crop us. You begin to feel more and more entrenched in an incorrect world surrounded by negative people.

You begin to feel the futility of your work, routine, and life. You may also begin to hate your routines but have no reason to break them. You begin to realize that routines are a necessity, and you are trapped in that cycle. You have just become a cog in the wheel and don't seem to find a purpose. It is the feeling that makes life look pointless.

It is important to understand that it is just a perception, and more, so your perception. The world may not believe in it. Even the person standing next to you may not believe in it, and hence there can be no reason for you to be sure that it is the truth.

Mental clutter has the power to play such games with your mind, and you will have to remain cautious of the things that originate in your mind.

Thoughts- Your Creation

A simple thing that most people fail to realize is that the thoughts that keep them traumatized to such an extent and make their lives difficult are their creation. In simple words, all the thoughts floating in your mind, pushing you towards negativity, fear, and anxiety and your creations, and you can rub them off. You can push your thoughts, mold them, bend them, or change them.

Elimination of the thoughts is not a possibility because that would mean compromising the functioning of the brain. Still, it is possible to identify thoughts as your own or to distance yourself from them.

Let us take one more example.

- You've had an altercation in your office
- People were witness to that altercation
- You suspect/know that your boss would get the news and would summon you

When you reach your home, you can take two lines of thought:

First

- The boss would hear about the news and would take it against you
- You will get a reprimand in the office tomorrow
- What if the boss begins to scold you in front of others
- What impression would that leave on others about you
- It'd be so difficult for you to face them
- What a shameful act would it be

- How would you be able to face your juniors
- It'd be so much better if you didn't work there
- You can even go to your boss early and ask for forgiveness for everything
- You can promise that you'll never repeat such a thing again

Second

- You had an altercation
- You were not at fault
- It was wrong for the other person to keep an unjust demand
- You'd tell your boss about the altercation and complain about the unjust treatment meted out to you
- You'd also tell your boss that proper chain of command was not followed
- You were given a task that was outside your job profile
- You'd also tell that you had agreed to do the job even then, but excessive pressure was put on you to finish it within impossible deadlines

As you can see, we took different approaches to deal with the same problem.

In the first one, the mind was cluttered with many insecurities. It was easy to drift away from the core issues. We could see that there was no focus, and the mind kept on exploring problems within the problem.

The infinite loop of thought that takes precedence can be very dangerous.

The more clutter you have in mind, the easy it would become for such loops to form.

In the next chapter, we will learn about the main causes of mental clutter.

Chapter 3: Why Our Brains Become Cluttered?

We can go on talking about the demerits of mental clutter because it is an inexhaustible topic. There is nothing more dangerous than a cluttered mind because it can obstruct your thought process. It can bend the way you think or look at things.

It can make you fearful, anxious, and even dangerous.

Mental clutter is not the right thing to have as it can change you as a person. A person with a highly cluttered mind can become more judgemental, suspicious, eccentric, and lunatic. The rest of us with moderate amounts of clutter lead our lives in an uneventful way, trying to find a way out of the loop.

But, have you pondered about the presence of this clutter in our minds?

Do you think that all the generations before us had the same amount of clutter?

Do you think that they also suffered like us?

Has mental clutter always existed in the same way?

Have we become more vulnerable to mental clutter?

Have you ever had such thoughts?

Mental clutter has always been there. Even our ancestors suffered from a lack of clarity of thought, hatred, jealousy, and other such problems resulting from mental clutter. Therefore, mental clutter has always been a problem in our race.

However, none of our ancestors had such a huge exposure to all kinds of information as we have. We live in a digital age where information is always at our fingertips, and hence we are taking in more than we can absorb.

We are always dealing with more stress because we concern ourselves with more things than we should. We are living in the most comfortable times our race has ever seen. There is much less to worry about bringing food to the table and finding shelter, and hence we begin to bother about things that do not even mean anything.

Comparatively, we live a life of abundance, and hence we are also naturally facing the problem of choice. We are forced to make choices all the time that can also add to the stress.

We have so much more than our ancestors, and yet we are worried about losing something precious. The current generation is living in Fear of Missing Out (FOMO).

We judge everything with our biases and then suffer from them.

All these things lead to more and more clutter in our minds. The more we think about these, the more clutter we accumulate.

To be specific, four things are cluttering the mind:

1. Stress
2. Decision Fatigue
3. Hoarding
4. Negative Thought Patterns

Stress

We Do Not Have a Reason to be Stressed

There has been no time in history when the Human Race had so much comfort and resources at the disposal.

- We are less vulnerable and dominate this blue planet

- Numerable gadgets, thanks to science and technology, are available to help us in all our chores
- Food security has never been this better
- There are better laws to govern societies, and most people in the world have a voice
- Healthcare has never been better. Even the most dreadful diseases have treatments or proper management arrangements. Even pandemics are unable to cause the same amount of havoc as they did in the past.

Despite All This, the Stress is a Stark Reality

You can't disagree that humankind has never lived in a more comfortable era in the past. Yet, it is undeniable that this generation's current stress levels are over the roof. Not only in adults but also among young kids, the stress levels are at an all-time high. The prognosis is very scary.

Stress, depression, anxiety disorders, panic attacks, and posttraumatic stress disorders are at their peak in our times. Some experts believe that even during the two world wars in the first half of the twentieth century, people's stress levels were not this high. Studies show that among the working adults, more than 73% face varying degrees of stress. People believe that desire to get a raise is the main reason behind most job switches these days. Data suggests otherwise. Experts believe that most people also switch their jobs as they want to break free of the workplace stress they were facing in their previous jobs. Yet, there is no proof that they can find the desired ease, even in their new jobs.

Stress- A Biological Response

Stress is an automated biological response created by the body to handle crises. The crisis can be a physical threat, an emotional trigger, and even an aggravating thought. Irrespective of the nature of the stress trigger, the reaction of the body is similar. It attempts to elevate some physical responses to be in a better position to cope with the imminent threat.

For instance, you face a stronger opponent at a secluded corner and realize that you will be attacked. You might be weaker, but the stress response in your body will increase your blood pressure, and your breath rate will increase. Your heart will begin to pump more oxygen to the muscles, and the blood sugar consumption by the cells would slow down so that your muscles have more sugar for prolonged performance. You may not be in an attacking position, but these changes will give you better output to evade the situation. You will be able to run much faster so that escape can be made. This unique mechanism makes stress response an integral part of our system. It helps us survive against all the odds. Even when our ancestors were facing stronger, fiercer, and faster beasts in the forests, this stress response gave them a better chance of survival.

Stress can be your savior when you are facing a do or die situation. The stress response to physical dangers is acute, and as soon as the crisis is over, the body releases hormones to calm down the whole system. It is a reason after a highly intense situation is over; you feel very tired and calm.

However, in modern times, such situations are few and far between. We are not facing such physical threats daily. Yet, we experience low-levels of stress most of the time. This stress is not helpful. On the contrary, this stress can cause serious damage.

Unusual Grounds for Stress

These days chronic stress much more prevalent than acute stress. It isn't the stress that leads to a sudden adrenaline rush in your veins and a deeper calm, succeeding that. You feel a little stressed all the time. You are not able to find peace of mind, and your stress receptors are always on alert. This stress is not strong enough to evoke a relaxation response but long and powerful enough to keep you feeling agitated. As a response to the stress, your body keeps releasing the stress hormone cortisol. This hormone has the power to disrupt several important functions in your body. It can cause insulin resistance, high blood pressure, obesity, high cholesterol, cardiovascular diseases, poor immune response, and several chronic inflammations.

People do not realize the things that can evoke a chronic stress response in their bodies. That's why it is such a rampant issue. Our generation is the most anxious, nervous, apprehensive, and stressed-out generation of all. We feel anxious about the most anxious things and want to brush them under the carpet.

- We get intimidated by the active life of our online friends and start feeling stressed. More often than not, social posts are presenting an unreal picture, and we know it. Yet, we remain stressed. Our mind remains cluttered. We keep feeling miserable.
- Simple choices in life can make us anxious. Ever felt anxiety in picking a cereal in a superstore? There is no reason to feel so, yet we keep questioning ourselves. We make simple decisions so important for ourselves.
- We keep aspiring for things that we don't even need. Success or failures shouldn't matter in such cases, but we make them a cause of stress.
- We let the outside influence of news, social media, and gossip affect our minds. Information overload is increasing the stress, and we are allowing it to do so.

Biologically, stress is not such an evil that we must bother about. It is a protective mechanism. However, excess of everything is bad, and stress can be no exception.

The real culprit here is the cluttered mind that gives way to unusual stress. The stress we face today is not real. It is the perception of threat that's causing all the damage.

Stress Can Have Physical Implications

Most people don't realize, but chronic stress can have physiological implications. Most of these problems are so common in their nature that they never raise eyebrows towards chronic stress. However, if you suffer from these regularly and are working in a stressful environment or have some nagging fear, you need to be more careful. Chronic stress can be the main culprit behind the problems.

Mild but chronic pain in your head and your limbs, indigestion, stiffness in muscles, sleep disorders like sleep apnea can be signaling the presence of chronic stress. Some emotional symptoms of stress can also be visible like irritability, bad temper, hopelessness, low sense of self-worth, self-pity, and inability to control mood swings.

Some of the Physical Symptoms of Stress are:

Clumsiness in Attitude, Rash, and Accident Prone Behavior

Stress is a result of clouded thinking. You keep miscalculating things and then make last-minute adjustments. It brings clumsiness in your behavior. Your decisions become rash and accident-prone. In most cases, these things happen when you try to bite more than you can chew. If you want to have everything on your plate at once, preventing the spilling gets difficult.

These days, people also try to give it the fancy name of multi-tasking. Our mind works best when it is focused on one thing at a time. Complete focus brings perfection. It reduces the chances of accidents and leads to better results. Your mind has a clear objective. It is the best way to deal with things. Taking one step at a time ensures that you are always on a strong footing and grounded. If you want to remove clumsiness from your attitude, clearing the clutter from your mind is very important.

Pain in Shoulders, Back, and Neck

Stress leads to some strange chemical reactions in our bodies. When you are stressed, alarmed, or anxious, your body starts releasing the stress hormones. These hormones create stiffness in your shoulders, neck, and back. These changes are designed to make you more resilient to damage in case of an attack. They made us better equipped to handle combat situations. However, in modern life, stress is not caused due to physical danger, but as a result of worries and anxieties. It lasts longer as your mind stays fixed on that problem. Prolonged stiffness brought by these circumstances leads to stiffness and pain in shoulders, back, and neck.

The best way to deal with this problem is to take short breaks. Deviate your mind from the current problem and indulge your mind into something else. The more relaxed you feel, the lesser the problem would be.

Tensions and Headaches

Stress has a profound impact on the brain. When you are in stressful situations, your heart-rate increases, breathing quickens, and your blood pressure rises. Your body starts pumping more blood and oxygen into your system to handle the problem. Prolonged exposure to this condition leads to the contraction of muscles, which lead to headaches.

Your mind would become foggy and would not be able to think clearly in such situations. Taking breaks in such situations is the best resort.

Diarrhea or Constipation, Indigestion, Ulcers, or Heartburn

Your mind and the rest of your body may look separate, but they are closely interconnected in reality. Stress not only causes problems to your brain but also transfers the information to the cells in your body. Your gut has more neurons than your spinal cord. Your gut produces a lot of acid in stressful situations. It leads to indigestion, ulcers, diarrhea or constipation, and heartburn.

Therefore, stress is not only a problem for your head but your gut too. If you are in a gut-wrenching situation or need to make a decision, which has put you in a fix, leave it aside for a few moments to cool down. Distracting yourself from the point for the moment helps in bringing clarity of thought.

Excessive Cravings for Stimulants like Caffeine, Cigarettes, and Change in Appetite

Excessive stress puts a heavy burden on your mind. It starts looking for stress relievers, and this is where caffeine, cigarettes, chocolates come into play. These things led to the release of stress-relieving neurotransmitters called dopamine and serotonin. They make you feel better. However, overdependence on these things can lead to addiction and cause potential damage.

Abusing these things is a symptomatic treatment and will have no long-term advantage. The best way always is to address the cause of the problem. Your high-stress level is the main problem, and till the reasons for high stress and not addressed, things won't change.

Disturbed Sleep, Insomnia, Nightmares

Sleep is one of the best stress busters. It helps your body in relaxing and releasing stress. However, when your mind is not at rest, sleep is a luxury you can't afford.

Stress has a strong impact on sleep patterns. People suffering from high stress have erratic sleep patterns and suffer from insomnia. If your mind is too cluttered, your subconscious will keep playing the same scary scenarios even in your sleep, and you can have nightmares.

This problem can only be resolved by consciously addressing the issues. The more you run away from the problem, the scarier they'll become. It would help if you prepared yourself to address the issues in reality. Please write down the problems you are facing in place of running them repeatedly in your mind. It clears some space in your mind and helps in removing the clutter. You can also discuss the problem with your family and friends as this gives the problem an outside perspective. Discussing it with others also helps you in coming out with a disclosure. The problems begin to scare you a bit less. If your stress affects your sleep, you should start acting quickly as the problem would escalate pretty soon. It will also affect you physically as well as emotionally. You will feel more tired and foggy due to lack of sleep and lose clarity of thought and energy.

Weight Gain

People normally associate weight gain with poor eating habits and bad food. However, abrupt weight gain also has its roots in high-stress levels. When you are under stress, your body releases a stress hormone called cortisol. This hormone sends your body in safe mode, and most of the weight loss functions stop working efficiently. It is one of the strongest reasons for sad or depressed people exhibiting significant weight changes. Stress also leads to emotional and compulsive eating that also helps in weight gain.

A significant increase in weight due to stress will start a vicious cycle. It would make shedding weight difficult and cause more weight-related stress. If you are experiencing weight gain and feel that your stress is a reason behind it, then start taking preventive measures right away. Create healthy distractions for yourself. Walking, exercise, yoga, swimming, and other such physical activities will not only help you in burning more fat, but they'll also help in distracting your mind from the stress.

Several other physical symptoms are related to stress like low energy levels, acne, dry skin, frequent infections, substance and drug abuse, and other addictions. All these things will keep pushing you in a corner towards more depression, anxiety, worries, and loneliness. Not attempting to get out of them isn't a solution.

Most of the stress is a result of muddled thinking. Your mind stops thinking rationally or gets pinned down in the wrong direction. A fresh start towards the problem can help in solving the problem. You can take a break from the problem.

Remember that stress doesn't only have physical symptoms but emotional ones too. It is working on your emotions too. The longer you remain under stress, the more difficult it will get to come out of it.

Some of the Emotional Symptoms of Stress are:

The feeling of Being Overwhelmed

Problems can start looking overwhelming. It can feel like that they have pinned you down. Feeling helpless under them will be of no use. Try hard to overcome them. Use affirmations to remind yourself that you can come out of stressful situations, and they aren't going to last long.

Feeling Sad or Hopeless

There will be times when the tunnel starts looking endless. However, nothing is endless in this world, not even the problems. All things come to an end, and so would your problems. Feeling sad or helpless only makes winning more and more difficult.

Irritability

Stress causes irritability, and that takes away your ability to rationalize. It is a bad move from all aspects. The more irritable you get, the more hostile and unreceptive environment you'll create for yourself. If you are becoming irritable, moving away from the problem for some time is the best solution.

The Feeling of Guilt and Worthlessness

Stress can lead to feelings of guilt and worthlessness. You will have to constantly remind yourself that the situation isn't permanent and doesn't define you. Positive affirmations and indulgence in something creative is the best way to overcome these negative feelings.

Becoming Oversensitive

Stressful situations make people oversensitive to comments. It creates more negativity. Your thinking gets muddy, and your decisions get mixed with ego. It is a negative response. Listening emphatically and understanding the situation is the right solution.

Procrastination

When you find something tough or challenging, the first response is to avoid it. However, in day-to-day life, many things can't be passed on that easily. People tend to delay such things indefinitely, and that leads to more problems. Procrastination is a cognitive effect of stress. Your flight response to the situation creates it. Not dealing with the problem wouldn't dilute its intensity, only decrease the time at hand to deal with it.

Stress is a Result, Not the Cause

Stress is causing a lot of problems. We all want to get rid of this stress and live a comfortable life. A whole new industry has sprung, which is trying to ease stress. But, is it effective? The answer is a resounding 'No.' It tries to treat the symptoms and not the causes.

Stress is simply a consequence of our misplaced priorities, unfulfilled desires, and negative thought patterns. The real cause of the problem is our Cluttered Mind. By the time you do not sort your aspirations, goals, and priorities, and the problems would remain in place.

Decluttering of the mind is crucial for getting actual relief from stress. When your mind is clear, you'll have better goals. Your aspirations from life would be more definite and rewarding. You will not succumb to the pressure and will have better ways to handle it.

If you want to lead a stress-free life, you will have to learn ways to manage your life more successfully. You cannot achieve this goal until and unless your mind starts to think clearly.

Shooting the Messenger

One of the biggest problems we face in problem-solving is that we are very quick to pass judgments. Chronic stress is a known issue. A large part of the population is a victim of chronic stress. However, we think by blaming the problems on the stress, they'll come to an end.

Some people who are more troubled by stress seek help in dealing with stress. They want to get a solution to stress by medication, therapy, or by intoxicating themselves. However, very few people are interested in addressing the cause of stress.

It would help if you remembered that you could take several measures to temporarily alleviate the symptoms of stress and may even get relief. But, that will not address the root cause.

The Stress is Not the Cause, But an Effect

A very important thing to understand is that the stress you face in your life and its ailments are not the cause of the problem but an effect of the mental clutter you already have. By focusing only on stress, you'll only hide the symptoms. The real problem would remain stationary at its place. It will even get a better chance at strengthening its roots within your mind.

The stress is only a response to the feelings and emotions you are experiencing at the moment. If your mind is calm and peaceful, there will be no stress. However, like stress, even these effects can be generated temporarily.

Some people heavily rely on alcohol, drugs, and other ways to intoxicate their minds. Their focus is to numb their ability to feel stress temporarily. They are successful to some extent, however short the period may be.

Another approach to dealing with stress is to seek medical treatment. Several therapeutic interventions can help you in keeping your stress levels low. They are only trying to numb your stress receptors chemically. It is like anesthesia to numb the pain.

Others seek more organic ways to address stress. They seek refuge in methods like deep breathing and meditation. Meditating for a while can help you in taking your mind away from stressful thoughts. Although deep breathing and meditation are a part of the decluttering process, if you use them as standalone procedures to instantly eliminate the stress, they will only work like other temporary measures.

Chronic stress is not the cause of the problem, and hence only dealing with stress is not going to yield anything. You would have to understand the deeper cause of the problem and help eliminate stress from your life.

Your focus must always remain on the decluttering of the mind. Chronic stress is the medium through which mental clutter manifests itself physically. You will have to take measures to deal with mental clutter to lower your overall chronic stress.

Once you have decluttered your mind and your thoughts, you will think with greater clarity. You will not feel burdened by your thoughts all the time. Hence, there will be no place for chronic stress.

Decision Fatigue

Decision fatigue is a contributor to stress in our daily lives. It results from the clutter around us, which leads to the compulsions to make decisions, even for unimportant things.

Every morning you have to think about which shirt you'll wear. Then you have to decide whether it'll look good on you. You also bother about that shirt, not looking loud or meek. You have to make so many decisions only for wearing a shirt that's hanging in front of you. The more shirts you have, the higher will be the compulsion to make decisions. The more decisions you are forced to make, the more you'll be taxing your active mind for useless reasons.

The active mind has a very important role to play. It needs to be alert and active for important decisions. The more you force it to bother about useless decisions, the more exhausted it will feel. It'll begin losing its sharpness and treat all decisions the same way.

The active mind is a resource that you can choose to waste on useless decisions and then feel entangled all the time, or you can conserve it for important ones and remain sharp.

Our ancestors had meager means. They had very few decisions to make. Most of the things in their lives were predetermined. Hence, the level of decision fatigue faced by them was low.

That's not the case with us. We are living in an age of abundance. You have hundreds or even thousands of choices in the food itself. It is why you face decision fatigue even while ordering food, which should be a fairly easy task.

Decision fatigue is sorely not a bad thing only because it makes us choose between things. It isn't good because it begins the chain of thoughts that will not stop.

Suppose you had eight shirts in your wardrobe that you could have worn that day. You picked a shirt after some deliberation. However, you made a choice, and there is no way you can be sure that you made the right choice because the decision is subjective, and your thoughts can challenge it. Your mind might wander on the topic that you should have picked the other one. The same indecision can crop up in terms of food. It can arise for deciding to go somewhere or buying or not buying something.

Whenever such thoughts arise, they begin probing possibilities, and that's the realm of assumptions.

The physical and mental clutter would always lead to decision fatigue, giving way to stress.

The more decisions you make, the more it will burden your mind. That's the reason people tasked with making important decisions try to avoid making useless ones.

Mark Zuckerberg, the CEO of Facebook, wears the same color of clothes to work daily. He says that it saves the trouble of making choices every day. Barak Obama had all his suits of only two colors. He believed that reducing the number of things to choose from helped ease the brain to use it for great importance decisions fully.

When we tax our brains to make continuous decisions, we force them to think quantitatively and not qualitatively. We are helping in the production of clutter, which will come back to us as problems.

If you want to lower stress and clutter in your life, you must work on lowering decision fatigue in your life.

Try to eliminate choices in things that you have to do daily. Fix things for specific days so that you can get variety but not have to make continuous days.

Hoarding of Thoughts and Memories

If anything, we are excellent hoarders. We like to accumulate things and cling to them. You might have seen that people have a lot more in their homes than they could use in two lifetimes.

An average American household has more than 300,000 items.

I don't think that you'll be surprised by this fact. More than 84% of the Americans worry that their homes aren't organized, and they have clutter. The percentage of Americans having mental clutter is much higher.

When it comes to mental clutter, we are even worse hoarders. Clearing physical clutter is easy. You can have a garage sale, and you can donate it to some charity, or pay someone to get rid of the clutter. Therefore, the chances are that someone else can help you in getting rid of the physical clutter.

However, things are not so easy with mental clutter.

Most of the mental clutter is present in the form of memories and the baggage of the past. People identify with those memories, and hence resist detachment from them. Getting off the past baggage is the most difficult, pushing them towards not doing anything to improve their situation or procrastination.

People remain fearful of a few things, and although there are ways to tackle those fears, people choose to live with them forever.

We accumulate fears, anxieties, insecurities, aspirations, fear of those failing in the end, and several other things in our minds. We keep them intact. We never move on. We never experiment. We do not deal with them.

Such things will lead to inactivity, procrastination, and will make you a sitting duck that can be shot easily at will.

Bear with me a small story again.

Once there was a farmer. He had a big farm, but he had bad luck in the past harvests. Sometimes the harvests got affected by droughts, and sometimes pest attacks killed the harvest. The farmer decided he had had enough of this nonsense. He wouldn't bear this nonsense again as his harvests were getting ruined anyway. So, he decided to play it safe and planted nothing. Was that a solution? It was not a solution. Earlier the farmer had a fear that his harvest would get affected by rain or pests. There was a possibility that he may not get the full harvest. But, his inactions made it a certainty that he will not get anything at all. Playing safe is sometimes the worst move. The baggage of the past does this to you.

If you let your mind and thoughts rule your world, then you will rot in a corner without ever seeing the light of the day. It will keep telling you that the world is full of dangers and risks.

Learning from past mistakes and letting it go is the only way to excel in this world. If your mind is cluttered with worries, it will never be able to learn and succeed. It will lack the required potential. A cluttered mind is never able to make the distinction between a safe decision and a fearful decision.

Safe decisions are based on reality. They have their basis on the possible consequences of decisions, and they invoke remedial precautions. The farmer could have made alternative irrigation arrangements. He could have employed pest control measures. Even if he hadn't done any of these, the probability of getting a harvest was 50-50. But, he took a fearful decision of doing nothing. The result was a guarantee of having nothing at all. Fearful decisions come from your insecurities, and they keep getting stronger. If you do not learn to fight them, they will degrade you and make you sub-human with no capability to enjoy this life.

Until we keep hoarding thoughts in mind and cling on to them, we will never be able to make rational decisions and be out of fear. We'll always feel anxious about things because our memory will tell us that something went wrong at one point in the past in a similar situation, and hence there is every possibility that things would go wrong even this time.

Getting over the baggage of the past is very important if you want to declutter your mind. It is easier said than done, but you must remain assured that it can be done. Memories of the past are intimidating, but they aren't invincible.

Negative Thought Patterns

Our negative thinking pattern is also a part of the survival mechanism. Earlier, the human race had bleak chances of development and survival. Our enemies were stronger and fiercer. We had to brave the natural forces and predators and didn't even have the natural defenses as most of the aminal kingdom species have.

Our ancestors had simple minds still in the developmental stage, and they didn't have the luxury to commit the same mistakes several times. Here, negative thought patterns played a very crucial role:

Carelessness Could Have Got Us Killed

Our ancestors couldn't afford to be careless. Mistakes in the wild mean elimination. They had to be alert all the time. They had to learn from all the misfortunes they had. The lessons were hard and painful.

Everything had to be learned and remembered from learning how to evade beasts to survive in extreme weather conditions. Careless was not an option. A highly conscious mind that keeps bringing problems in front of you and never lets your insecurities calm down is a part of that system itself.

Negative Thought Patterns Kept Us Alert

The function of negative thought patterns is to keep us alert. It never allows us to forget what can be troublesome. If you feel that you can fall from a ledge and die, you will have a numbing fear when you go near it. You would feel as if you are going to fall at any moment. This mechanism has been in place to keep you in a complete alert mode when we sense danger.

Our ancestors faced physical threats that didn't last very long or were not chronic. These days the threats are different.

You could be worried that your boss is going to scold, punish, penalize, or fire you the next morning. There is no physical threat. However, because there is no proximity threat, you could be worried about it even weeks, days, and hours before it happens.

Your mind will remain fixated on the thought and will not think anything at all. It will begin the vicious cycle of mental clutter resulting in chronic stress.

The more you think about it, the more stressed you'll feel, and therefore, the more you'll think about it. It is an eternal cycle.

Negative Thought Patterns Are Based On Your Threat Perception

Negative thought patterns do not have their intensity. They are always based on your threat perception. If you believe that the chances of something happening are high and you are fearful of severe consequences, the negative thought process will be very intense.

It is your threat perception that gives power to negative thought patterns. Managing them may be well within your reach if you can analyze the threat perception logically or rationally.

If you keep exciting the threat perception, your negative thought pattern may have no end to it.

Numbing fear all the time is irrational

Most people experience a numbing fear even when they are not in imminent danger. They are not able to break their chain of thoughts and keep on repeating the same fearful thoughts. It can be a very dangerous thing to do.

Most of the time, when you are not facing a physical threat, there is no need for numbing fear. You are in a position to make a rational decision and plans to avert the situation.

However, fear can make them indecisive, which leads to inaction. It significantly lowers the chances of avoiding problems.

Indecision, Irrationality, Fright, and Weakness

These are some of the common emotions people feel when negative thought patterns bound them. What makes negative thought patterns so dangerous is the fact that they feed on your insecurities.

The more fearful thoughts you have in your mind, the stronger will be the chain of thoughts.

Fighting them or getting out of them can become very difficult because mental clutter will constantly fuel it. It will evoke a stress response, and you will keep sinking deep.

Repetition of The Same Thoughts Over And Over Again

As I have discussed, negative thoughts keep playing over and over in your mind. You have no respite from those thoughts. No matter how hard you try to evade them, they are in your mind. The fear will keep getting intensified.

It isn't a random process. Your subconscious mind is playing such thoughts on a loop to make you conscious of the danger or the threat perception you have. It may look like a passive process, but it isn't.

You will Have To Become Conscious Of The Negative Thought Patterns

The way to break these negative thought patterns is to become conscious of your thoughts. You will have to become aware of your thoughts and make conscious efforts to push them aside. You will also have to address the causes behind those thoughts' emergence and address even those causes.

All of this will require a conscious understanding and effort. You will have to work systematically to declutter your thoughts. But, before you do that, you must identify the clutter in your mind and understand the reasons behind all the muck that's getting thrown from one side to another in the form of negative thoughts.

Chapter 4: The 8 Common Symptoms of Clutter

A cluttered mind is not difficult to spot. Mental clutter makes the person clumsy and adds various adjectives to the personality like indecision, confusion, cynicism, criticism, judgementalism, isolation, and many others.

A person with a lot of stress and anxiety at the back of the mind never lives easy.

However, have you heard that there is darkness under the lamp?

While you may find it very easy to stop the signs of mental clutter in others, identifying and admitting that even you suffer from the same malice can be a tall order.

Most people like to evade the question as they like to evade other unpleasant thoughts in their lives and, as a result, suffer all their lives. Stress, anxiety, confusion, procrastination, hesitation, and many other similar issues become a regular feature of their lives.

The option to run from the question and keep suffering or look for the answer and seek peace is always there with you.

We all suffer from varying degrees of mental clutter. The rate of accumulation of mental clutter also differs from person to person. Some people are highly anxious, and they begin to absorb every piece of information as a survival need. They are likely to accumulate much more clutter.

Others are more composed, and they exercise greater control in absorbing information. Such people are less likely to accumulate more clutter.

Everyone must try to evaluate whether their minds are clutter or not. It is important to know that like every other good or bad habit, and even clutter accumulation is also a habit. If you keep accumulating clutter for very long, it becomes a part of your habit. You'd find it hard to get over it.

Eight common symptoms can help you identify whether you have excess clutter in your mind or not.

They are:

Lack of Clarity: A cluttered mind is usually foggy. There is so much going inside such a mind at any time that it is always difficult to focus completely on any one thing. It is the reason people with cluttered mind lack clarity of thought or remain confused.

Here, it is important to remember that it is not the storage space that's the evil, but the difficult retrieval part. You can keep storing any amount of information in your mind, but that doesn't mean you'll be able to recall all of it when needed. For that, you'll need to be specific and create dedicated memories.

The higher the information overload you experience, the greater would be the confusion in your mind. Higher information overload would mean that some part of your brain would get triggered at every instance of receiving information and want to contribute. Still, there will not be a clarity of the kind of information you have.

It is similar to spotting a known face and then worrying all the time who that was. We all have experienced this in our lives. Some faces look familiar, and we struggle hard to place a name to that face. The result is fatigue as we seldom succeed.

It doesn't do any harm to that person, but your mind becomes fatigued. Now, think of that happening with your mind all the time when it keeps getting triggered by every bit of information.

Lack of clarity or mental confusion is a big sign that your mind is getting cluttered and struggling with placing information properly. Information overload is a big reason behind this problem, but there can also be several other factors.

Mind Chatter: Our mind is never static. It is fluid and volatile. There is a lot of electrical activity going inside the brain. These electrical impulses carry thoughts and memories.

Our brain has around 100 billion neurons, and every neuron has around 15,000 connections. As you can see, we have already started talking trillions.

Hence, mental chatter is a continuous process for every individual on this blue ball called earth. However, people with more mental clutter will have more things to get transported for processing. The chatter will be louder in their minds.

A person with mental clutter would suffer from a lack of focus and attention. Such people would always remain distracted and lost. They'd find it very hard to focus on anything, even for a few seconds.

It is the story of the current age. While the baby boomers had an attention span of minutes, the millennials only have an attention span of 12 seconds. It isn't all; Generation Z or the current generation has an even shorter span of 8 seconds. It seems as if the whole generation is suffering from ADHD.

People are simply absorbing more and more information without paying attention to the kind of information they are soaking in. It is going to create a mind chatter that you are unable to understand.

A cluttered person will have too many thoughts in mind and too little focus. Paying attention to anything for very long will be very difficult for such individuals. They'll be fidgety and keep shifting from one topic to another as if trying to find a balance.

Excessive mind chatter can be a disruptive force as it makes it difficult to be at peace. You keep having thoughts even when you don't want them. It seems as if you are suffering from some mental diarrhea.

Now the reason for diarrhea is simple. If you have bad food, you'll have an upset stomach. The solution is even simpler. You'd need to give some rest to your processing center.

If you think you or someone else you know is also suffering from mental chatter, identifying mental clutter shouldn't be a difficult task.

Constant Conflict: A person with mental clutter is never at peace. There is always dissent about the thoughts and ideas created by the mind or held by others. Mental clutter can lead to chaos and disorganization in the mind.

The mind always finds it hard to agree to some specific point. There are always thoughts, memories, ideas, and information that would form a conflicting opinion.

It can be a good thing for debates, but when it becomes a regular feature of your personality or nature, it can present several issues.

People with mental clutter always find it hard to conclude. They'll always doubt in their minds. They'll never be sure of anything.

Such people find it difficult to agree with others and have difficulty making a firm decision. They keep rocking back and forth on every decision.

Seek Validation: Mental clutter makes it difficult for a person to become confident about anything, and hence such people seek validation for everything. You may think that this is a good thing, but it isn't.

Mental clutter makes such people look for validation, but it also makes them suspicious of others, and hence they don't easily trust others and their validation either.

As a result, they begin hoarding a lot more information and sources to validate their thoughts.

The mental clutter within them keeps piling up.

Collecting information and accolades become a favorite hobby of such people, and they keep flaunting these for regaining validation.

You'd find such people in urgent need of approval whenever they are telling anything. Even a little disapproval or disagreement can aggravate and excite such people easily.

Judgemental: It is another distinguishing trait of a person with too much mental clutter. When you have too much reference point stored in your mind, you begin to size up even those that don't need your approval.

People with mental clutter can be seen commenting on others, or they keep thinking about how others behave, talk, dress, or conduct themselves. They may give their opinion even when no one has asked for it

Constant comparisons are a part of the habit for such people.

It is something dangerous that begins to develop in their mind. The comparisons they create for others become insecurities for themselves. They are also constantly trying to see if they fit the perfect standard or not, and believe me, most of the time, anyone would fail. It renders them shaken, underconfident, and sullen.

You can easily spot such individuals with the kind of judgemental attitude they possess.

Bite More Than They Can Chew: It might look like an uncanny quality, but it isn't. We all plan and allocate time and energy for things. Such people go on overdrive while doing this. They'll always commit more that they can afford.

They'll always have more engagements. They'll bear more responsibilities. They'll bear more burden than they can carry.

Their minds are always full, and hence they can't take things slow. But that's not a good thing when they aren't able to carry anything to its fruition.

Such people are always at odds with others, relationships, family, work, finances, projects, and assignments.

They'll be seen failing in their commitments, procrastinating, and then blaming others for their failures.

Putting Conditions: This is another signifying trait of people with mental clutter. Such people would keep putting conditions after conditions for things to happen their way.

They'll not try to find their way around problems but figure out conditions that may have led to their failures. They'd keep blaming on a thing or the other for the things they couldn't do.

They couldn't rise in their office because they didn't have the right boos. They couldn't succeed in relationships because they didn't get the right partners, and so forth.

It seems as if all the misfortune has been striking them with precision.

In reality, like is never a cakewalk for most of us. We all have our struggles, and we have to overcome the obstacles we face.

Most people do not like to hide behind pretenses, but that's easy for people with mental clutter as their mind is on overdrive, creating such conditions and excuses.

Desire to Control: Mental clutter can fill you with a desire to have control. While a person has a lot of mental clutter and experiences complete anarchy in mind, it is common to have the desire to control all the things that can bring short order.

It is a desperate attempt to manage things and keep them in order. It is only an outward attempt and never directed inwards.

The more anarchy and disruption a person feels within, the stronger the desire to have control outside gets.

Therefore if you are looking at a control freak trying laboriously to manage things outside, you can be sure that the person has a very hard time managing the mind. It is just an attempt to avoid unpleasant surprises that may lead to more anarchy.

These eight symptoms are not very hard to detect. You can easily find these traits in any person you lay your eyes on. However, these are very hard to visualize when you are looking inwards.

Most of us never look inwards or are scared of looking inwards as we are scared of the things we may find. However, escapism can't take us anywhere, and the accumulation of mental clutter is also a result of this escapist routine.

You shouldn't be surprised if you look inwards and find a couple of these symptoms within yourself. We all have clutter in our minds, and we need to deal with it. We are not even debating the clutter's presence, as a very high number of us will have this clutter.

The amount of information overload we face, the society we live in, and the burden of expectations and responsibilities we bear will lead to mental clutter.

It'll be ideal if we didn't have any mental clutter, but that is something that you can't control.

You'll need to live in a controlled environment with highly disciplined individuals for having a spotless mind.

Gautama Buddha, the founder of Buddhism, was born to a king. When he was born, the astronomers told the king that either the child would become a great king or a great sage.

It worried the king greatly. He didn't want his only son to roam in the jungles with an empty belly. He asked the sages to tell the way to prevent him from becoming a sage.

The astrologer told that he could prevent his son from witnessing the pain, misery, and suffering in this world, which would keep him tied to the material world.

The king followed the instructions to the letter.

He ensured that his son never saw any old, sick, poor, injured, or dead person.

He remained in a very happy environment and became a young man. He was married and even had a son.

However, he was a prince of that state and the future ruler, and keeping him in the palace forever wasn't possible.

Gautama started going out, and one day, he saw and sick person.

Others saw an older person with a bent back walking on the road with great difficultly.

Then he also saw a dead person.

The pain, misery, and suffering of the world weren't hidden anymore from his eyes, and it made him question all that from within.

Soon enough, Buddha left his home in search of the answers for the suffering in the world.

Buddha roamed thousands of kilometers for years but found the truth and enlightenment sitting under a tree.

Buddha's story tells us that having a spotless mind was not possible even for kings, even in those times when there was no unrestricted flow of information. In the current age, it is an impossibility.

However, there is a way to keep your mind spotlessly clean, which is the way of the Buddha.

Meditation, self-exploration, and seeking the truth within can help you cut the clutter and find what matters in reality.

You must understand that our brain is equipped to handle a good amount of clutter on its own. It is only the excess that creates the problems.

If you want to lead a life where you are not bothered by every thought you have or every problem that comes in front of you, then meditation, mindfulness, and decluttering of the mind are the techniques that can help you go a long way ahead.

Chapter 5: Why Mental Clutter is Even More Dangerous Than We Think?

Mental clutter is the fog that curtails your view. By itself, the fog may not seem to pose any danger to you. It can't choke, blind, or impede you, but we all know that the same fog can lead to life-threatening accidents.

None of us minds a little fog in our lives. You get up early in the morning, and there's a little fog outside, it doesn't bother you. You know it very well that after a while, there'll be enough sunlight to drive away all the fog, and there'll be clarity.

However, if the day is cloudy and cold and you have to drive down a risky road, you'll be bothered.

In the same way, some confusion or indecision about something may be of little consequence to you. However, the same can cause great havoc if the subject is of some importance or if you are in a state of panic.

In this era, the fog is all around us, and there is no hope of light coming from the outside. There is so much fog in our minds due to information overload that moving ahead will become dangerous and slow if we do not have clarity.

Unfortunately, mental clutter is still not an issue of great concern for most people. They think that it is a temporary state like a morning hangover after a night of heavy drinking. People believe that it'll go away. Their fears and anxieties about the things that concern them will fade away on their own. Little do they know that such things will not go away. All that is clutter, and it'll keep floating at the back of your mind clouding your decisions and functioning.

Everything from our hopes, aspirations, desires, longings, needs, loathing, failures, to our dreams, keeps looming large on our conscience. It not only affects our decision-making process but also alters the way you behave and lead your life.

Mental clutter has a deep and defining impact on your thought process, health, and the quality of life you lead.

It is the reason ignoring mental clutter can be detrimental. It has a ripple effect on the mind. The impact may not be evident initially, but as it proceeds further the intensity increases.

Five Main Areas Affected by Mental Clutter:

Impact on Thoughts: We have already discussed enough that mental clutter is the main cause behind all the stress, lack of focus, procrastination, fear, anxiety, and despair in life. The more mental clutter you have, the higher the percentage of stress, mental fog, and confusion in life.

You'll not focus on your goals, have a hard time fulfilling commitments, and find it excessively difficult to stick to major decisions. Mental clutter makes you anxious and fearful. Anger and frustration are the usual fronts that open up. People try to hide their inability to make decisions by exhibiting anger in exasperation. However, deep within, you always know that you are never in control of the situation.

Has it ever happened to you that you are trying to find a dress for the day in the morning and get frustrated that you have nothing to wear? Have you given it a thought that you are standing in front of a wardrobe?

In reality, you do not lack clothes but suffer from indecision. Type of clothes can never have such an important role in your life unless you are about to walk on a ramp, and in that case, the clothes won't be your problem.

Your problem is that your mind is cluttered with all the opinions you might have heard in various instances. A colleague's comment on a specific dress, not getting proper attention in another, or things like these always impact your mind. While you may not be thinking actively about these instances, every time you stand in front of the wardrobe, such thoughts in your subconscious begin to dominate your thought process.

Decision fatigue faced during dressing up is just an example taken for the sake of simplicity. We come face to face with such decisions all the time. They take up our energy and make us feel defeated at every step of the way.

The amount of indecision, anguish, anxiety, desperation, and despair you face depends on the amount of mental clutter in your mind. The higher the mental clutter in life, the more puzzled you'll feel.

Impact on Health: It is an aspect that never garners the attention it deserves. Most people keep blaming stress, anxiety, and frustration in their lives for all the health troubles they have. No one pays attention to the fact that mental clutter is the main cause of stress in their lives.

You may keep watching as many comedies as you may like or take as many vacations as you can afford, but until you understand that the stress you face is caused by mental clutter, these solutions are not going to work. You can take your eyes off stressful things, but you can't drive their thoughts out of your mind. Your mental clutter would not allow you to be at peace. It is the reason many people feel even more anxious when they are away from work.

You can keep on lowering the fat intake in your diet to keep your heart healthy, but if the mental clutter is pumping more and more cortisol in your blood, your diet management will not work. Diet changes will only become a coping mechanism, and nothing concrete will happen in reality.

From allergies to various kinds of sensitivities, mental clutter can manifest itself in the form of various health issues.

Impact on Relationships: We have more time on our hands than ever. Most of the things in our homes are automated. Yet, we have the least amount of time for our loved one these days. It is the reason the fabric of relationships is getting so weak.

Most people are never able to understand the reason for trouble in their relationships. They keep blaming their partners for whatever problems that may have arisen.

If you think that relationships can only be ideal between two individuals who are perfect for each other, you are gravely mistaken. The relationship is the fabric that keeps two distinct individuals tied together. However, it requires understanding, receptiveness, and tolerance. You can't have them until there is mental clutter.

We all want to be assertive; we want to be heard and understood. Yet, we stop listening. We keep recording every minor instance and then use it for judging the partner and expect the relationship to last long. These are unreal expectations, and they are bound to make relationships brittle.

Mental clutter leads to opacity. It inhibits the clarity of mind that is needed to understand the partner and empathize.

Mental clutter can jeopardize your love life and create differences with your kids. When dealing with relationships, we need to understand that we are dealing with human beings who think, feel, and perceive the situation, and that might be different from what you have in your mind.

Mental clutter comes in the way of this clarity, and rifts arise faster than you can think.

Impact on Career: Mental clutter is one of the biggest reasons behind procrastination, hoarding of work, and lack of clarity in communication. Any of the three is enough to kill an individual's career or make survival arduous, especially in a competitive organization.

If you think, somehow, you are missing your deadlines again and again, or you are getting more work than you can handle, you might be the one sitting in the hot seat.

Mental clutter makes you fear the work and also shirk from it. It is always an obstacle. It never allows you to have a clear view of your objective. But it always keeps the fear alive in your mind. It is the reason people keep piling up more and more work, but they are never able to finish it on time. Procrastination becomes their second nature.

It is easy to shift the blame on someone else's shoulders. It is natural for anyone to try to avoid the idea that they are suffering from mental clutter. However, the data tells otherwise.

As per data given by the Conference Board, around 53 percent of the Americans are unhappy at work. It is a majority number. Therefore, even if you felt the same, you'd need to stop feeling awkward and accept the problem.

Perception is a dangerous thing. Reports say that around 89 percent of the employers or the managers think that employees change their jobs for money. However, the actual percentage of employees changing jobs solely for a raise is just 12 percent. Around 79 percent of employees change their jobs because they think that they are not getting due appreciation.

The longing to get appreciation or validation from others is proof that you are suffering from mental clutter.

Mental clutter is not something that only affects you. It is a widespread issue. But make no mistake, no one will sympathize with you for it or understand it. It is something that only you have to suffer or overcome.

Impact on Quality of Life: Quality of life is an aspect that we always overlook when it comes to mental clutter. The clutter seeps into our lives in such subtle ways that we never realize its drastic impact.

As a child, we are all fearless, blissful, and full of life. We do not need anything to make us happy. If you look back, you'd realize that force was needed to make us unhappy. We could make a game out of anything and find reasons to be happy. Kids are never able to understand why adults are always so much stressed all the time. This blissfulness is there because a child is not identified with anything. There is no pressure, aspiration, expectation, or longing.

However, as we grow, all these things come into our lives and make us fearful. They clutter our lives and make us anxious. We get identified with so many things that we become conscious of everything and forget being carefree.

It has a deep impact not only on various important aspects of our lives but also as a whole on our lives.

Our lives may look good and comfortable from the outside, but we are always filled with fear, regret, and anxiety. We can never live our lives to its fullest extent because we are worried about what others would think of us. We begin living our lives as per the standards set by society.

Getting rid of mental clutter is important to get hold of life back.

If you do not learn to deal with the mental clutter, you may go on leading a life like others that may seem normal from the outside but will always be full of turmoil and discontent.

- You may keep doing things and have regrets
- You may associate yourself with people and loath them
- You may keep displaying a cheerful face and resent every moment of it
- You may keep changing jobs but never find a place where you could enjoy working

You struggle not because the world is against you but because your mind is your adversary. There is no way you can avoid your mind or run away from it.

Decluttering your mind is the only real way to get out of this mess. Before you ask for peace from the outside world, you'll need to ensure that there is peace within. If there is no peace within you, outside calm will have no meaning for you.

We need to understand that we are not worried about the outside noise. We have developed several measures to cut out the outside world's noises, but we have not worked much on our mind chatter.

You must have wondered:

- Why is your mind straying on various other things every time you try to focus on something important?
- Why does your mind keep projecting fear even during situations when it isn't warranted?
- Why is it so hard for people to even pray with complete focus?
- Why does their mind keep wandering here and there when they are trying to connect to the almighty?
- Why is peace such a difficult commodity in our times?

Constant bombarding of thoughts is the main culprit in all these instances. We all know that every time we try to focus on anything, our mind brings various other things. There is never real clarity of thoughts. There is commotion.

Let us get back to our traffic analogy once again.

Why do traffic jams occur?

Don't we have roads to accommodate all those cars?

It isn't a lack of roads but disorganization, disorder, and noncompliance, leading to traffic jams.

The same is the case of mental clutter and constant bombarding of thoughts. We have allowed our mind to go astray. We have never tried to discipline it. We have attached too much importance to our thoughts. Now, our thoughts have gained complete control of our being, and they have become unruly.

We are not struggling with the problem of capacity but order. Bringing calm and order in our mind should be our main objective, and decluttering the mind is the first step in that direction.

Chapter 6: Can We Stop the Constant Chatter of Thoughts in the Mind?

Peace of Mind is an Incorrect Objective

It is a sad and strange thing that our main objective is peace of mind today. After all that we do or achieve in our lives, we are ready to give up everything for peace of mind.

Peace of mind has never been an objective of humankind; it has always been quality.

From time immemorial, the human race has been striving for betterment. It has been trying to achieve something better than it had. It is the mindset that has made us better than all the other species in the world. We can think, observe, and critically analyze. Yet, we have made it a goal to put a stop to our power to think. The quest for peace is nothing more than this.

Our thoughts are the creation of our mind. No one has the power to put thoughts in our mind forcibly. Even if someone puts thoughts in our minds, whatever happens with those thoughts is our domain. Yet, a large portion of humanity is troubled because it cannot control the commotion of thoughts in mind.

It is a very grim situation. Not because irreversible but because we are not trying to change it.

Thoughtlessness is Impossible

People keep using fancy terminologies like thoughtlessness, no-mind, and peace of mind as if they have real meaning. For humanity, there can be no such thing as thoughtlessness.

If you want to achieve a state of complete thoughtlessness, you must have some serious prejudice against intelligence.

You must understand that the ability to think has not come to us without effort. It is a result of millions of years of evolution. Our minds can think even when it is in a subconscious state. We can't even think of designing a machine that can do its work even when switched off.

The whole concept of thoughtlessness is a sham.

It would be best if you understood in the beginning that you could never become thoughtless. You can never make your mind stop having thoughts. For that, you'd have to make the mind stop. In medical terms, that is called death.

However, does that mean you can never get rid of mental chatter?

Of course not!

Mental chatter and thoughtlessness are two very different things, and people usually get confused.

Bring Clarity Between the Conscious and the Subconscious Mind

We have a conscious mind and a subconscious mind. The conscious brain is the active brain that you can command; the subconscious is the latent part of the brain over which you have no control.

Our conscious mind does problem-solving and decision-making. These are slow and energy-consuming processes. No wonder, the brain even being such a small organ by mass, consumes a total of 20 percent of all the energy consumed by you.

You use the conscious brain to make a conscious judgment about things, make decisions, solve complicated problems, cater to various issues, etc.

All these things require analysis and assessment.

However, the scope of the conscious brain is very limited. It is active only when you are awake, and your thought process impacts your conscious brain's functioning. It means that your subconscious brain has an important role to play even here.

The scope of our subconscious brain is wide. It is the brain that is active 24 hours of the day. Even when a person is asleep or even in a comma, the subconscious brain is active. It has a very crucial role to play in our lives.

The subconscious process takes care of:

- Basic Life functioning
- Fight or flight response
- Behaviors and habits

You do not need to think about these things. These things happen as if you are on autopilot. A fun fact, 95 percent of all our actions are happening on autopilot. You don't need to think. When you change gears in your car or hit the brakes, you don't consciously think about it. Your body does that on its own. It happens on impulse. The subconscious brain sends these impulses.

Subconscious stores and records knowledge. It is the memory bank. Your observations, feelings, and experiences get recorded in the subconscious brain. It uses these memories to develop behaviors, habits, and impulses.

It is the job of the subconscious brain to take you away from pain and towards pleasure. The subconscious mind begins to label things, emotions, and experiences as good or bad, influencing our habits and behaviors to make this possible.

It makes you dream things and keeps some memories fresh.

However, the subconscious is not without faults. It is driven by the idea of keeping you safe and away from pain, and that is not always the best strategy to adopt. While it drives you away from danger, it keeps the danger fresh in your mind filling you with fear and anxiety. It is a form of survival mechanism—all the memories and experiences stored in the subconscious act as references.

You can choose to live in autopilot mode as it is an easy way. Less labor is required, and it is easy to navigate. However, it has its pitfalls.

The more you rely on the subconscious brain, the more you become a slave of habits. You begin to lose active control of our conscious brain. The thoughts produced with the help of memories stored in the subconscious begin to dominate our thinking patterns and actions.

It ultimately leads to mental chatter that you can never stop.

You are not troubled because there are too many thoughts in your mind, but you have no active control over them. As you begin to live your life on autopilot, you lose the agility to navigate on your own.

Any attempt to stop thoughts in your mind is futile because there is no way you can stop your subconscious brain. But, if you also lose control of your active brain, mental chatter and clutter will become a reality for you.

If you want to stop mental chatter from haunting you every waking moment of your life, you will have to learn to gain control of your active brain.

You will Need to Be Systematic

Most of us feel that mental chatter is chaotic and unsettling. However, very few are keen to investigate the cause. If you think carefully, you'll find that all thoughts are not equally bad. Some thoughts are troubling, some mean, some just bad, and some are even good.

You'd feel no need to deal with the good thoughts, but you are troubled by the other kinds of thoughts. It is natural to feel so. However, there is no way you can keep the good thoughts coming and stop the bad thoughts from influencing your life. You need to understand that the source is the same, and as long as you permit one, the other will have equal access.

Your subconscious mind is a storehouse of information. The more information you grasp, the larger the storage of memories, pictures, references, and the thoughts.

There is no filter for thoughts in the subconscious. The memories stored in the subconscious keep getting bounced randomly. However, you might have witnessed that the number of dreadful thoughts is always higher than good thoughts. There is a science behind it.

Our brain is programmed to keep you prepared for all kinds of eventualities, and that makes it necessary that you always remain on alert. That's the reason you keep getting negative thoughts so that you never get complacent.

Your past is stored in your subconscious. Every poor memory is stored as some fear or anxiety. Your weaknesses would keep coming back to you as your insecurities. They work as a means to push you toward improvement and recovery.

If you've had traumatic experiences in the past, the subconscious mind will ensure that you keep getting reflections of those events. It is again a measure to ensure that you don't become complacent. The memory flashbacks serve the specific purpose of keeping you alarmed about such events in the future.

In the life of our ancestors living without any means of protection or support, it meant everything. It helped them remain alarmed and stay away from dangers. This mechanism has helped humankind survive in the harshest living conditions and excel over the more powerful, fast, and ferocious beasts.

However, in this era, when the threat perceptions are low, you do not need that injection of threat all the time. But the mechanism that has evolved over millions of years wouldn't stop functioning all of a sudden. It is here to stay for some time. However, to a great extent, it is like the appendix now. An organ that is not needed anymore.

Ours is the most comfortable generation that has ever walked on this earth. We do not need to remain alert and awake every moment of natural threats that our ancestors faced. We can work best when our mind is positive and relaxed.

People know that they are at their productive best when their mind is focused and calm. They can achieve more when they are not thinking about a thousand things at the same time. We all know this, but the problem is that our subconscious mind is hard to train, and it keeps pushing us on the autopilot mode.

- Have you ever noticed the itch to do something else while watching TV or doing something else?
- Do you feel the need to watch TV or scan your phone while having food?
- Do you keep fidgeting silently while in a meeting?
- Do you keep moving the pen in your fingers, shake your legs, tap your feet silently, or do other such things even when listening to something important?
- Do you feel the itch to do something or check your phone even when you are watching something interesting?

- Do you love to multitask?
- Do you find it hard to focus only on one thing?
- Do you like to collect too many tasks to be completed in the day?
- Do you begin thinking about other things while talking to someone you don't particularly like?
- Do you think you are distracted most of the time?

If you answered a 'yes' to some of these, you must know that even you are running on autopilot. If you think that there can be a way to stop the mental chatter while being on autopilot, you are mistaken.

Mental chatter is not the cause of the problem but a result of the mental clutter you have. The mental clutter makes the subconscious mind evoke memories. The more the inflow of information to the subconscious, the greater the mental chatter.

You must understand that your mind is not the problem. Even the mental chatter is not the problem. Your problem is that most of the mental chatter you have is fearful, making you anxious. It reminds you of all your shortcomings or the missed opportunities you've had in life. Negative thoughts are your problem.

However, it would help if you also kept in mind that positive or negative mental chatter is only a reflection of the information you are taking in. Your mind is not creating those memories. It is only a storehouse. All the memories, thoughts, or feelings you get are just reflections of the information you are taking in.

If you are absorbing negative information, you are more likely to have negative thoughts. If you are a fan of horror movies, you cannot complain about the jump scares you get in the movie hall and your real life. It is a misconception that you can leave that movie behind in the cinema hall. It doesn't work like that. You have given fodder to your subconscious. It will now replicate those thoughts and images and fill that fear deep inside your heart as every image is a lesson.

You are bound to have indigestion if you are eating bad food.

It is a basic problem that people fail to understand in their lives, and they keep looking for solutions at all the wrong places. If you are giving your mind food for thought, you are bound to have the processed material as mental clutter.

The mind is a mirror. It will reflect everything that's inside. The pictures are always running randomly. From the faintest memories of your childhood to current events, everything has an imprint. Your subconscious keeps picking and flashing them up.

You have two options:

- Carefully Choose What You Ingest
- Use Your Mind Consciously

Carefully Choose What You Ingest

Information overload is a real problem that the current generation is facing. It can cause several complications. We are ingesting all kinds of information that we might need or not. There is no control or check. Although our mind has unlimited storage capacity, useless information will not add anything but only lead to mental clutter.

You are not responsible for this tendency of uncontrolled absorption of information. From our education system to our society, hoarding more and more information is considered quality. People are lauded for having encyclopedic memory.

However, people forget that although memorizing information in the past when there were no means of storing information in the written form was the norm. It is a waste of resources in the current age. We live in a world where you can store the needed data on various devices and even cloud storage. Much more data can be stored on these devices than you can ever recall when needed. Engaging your mind in a futile activity will only impact its productivity and efficiency.

The problem doesn't end here. The information we pick up from social media platforms, entertainment mediums, and the news also have a corrupting influence. Such information is neither useful nor productive; it is pure clutter.

We have started treating garbage as information. We have also started losing the power of discernment when absorbing any information. It is why advertisement companies, social media influencers, and the internet's content can influence our thought process, our buying choices, and our decisions so heavily.

Practically, we have stopped moving on our own; we are being led or driven by others.

It is a scary scenario because when someone else begins to make decisions for you, the active brain becomes even idler, and the mental chatter would increase.

If you are ingesting too much bad food, indigestion is an eventuality. Some people have a better digestive system and slow intake. They can avoid mental clutter for longer. Others are vice-versa, and they begin to face the symptoms soon. However, no matter how strong your digestive system is, if you are consuming unfiltered trash in an unrestricted manner, you will get sick.

If you feel that the mental clutter is giving you sleepless nights or deteriorating your productivity, first, you will have to manage the kind of information you are consuming.

The company you have, the kind of people surrounding you, the kind of discussions you participate in, the kind of programs you watch, and other such things have a deep impact on your thoughts.

If you are in a good company and having positive discussions, there is no reason for you to have negative thoughts. Positive mind chatter never bothers anyone. It doesn't even get registered by your mind because it isn't stimulated.

The real trouble begins when negative thoughts begin to stimulate your brain to take preventive action.

Therefore, you need to understand that you are not troubled by mental chatter per se, but by the negative chatter that keeps you overstimulated. It makes you feel insecure, anxious, and frightened.

The first way to do that is to stop absorbing information without filters. You'd need to deploy better filters when it comes to picking information.

We are simply acting like a sponge. We absorb anything that comes our way, which is why all the clutter in our minds. We'll have to learn to deal with that. Being mindful is a way to deal with the negativity that may come our way, and we'll be in a much better position to deal with negativity.

Socrates was a renowned philosopher in ancient Greece (469-399 BC). He is a man who is still known for his wisdom. He had a great strategy for allowing only useful information to pass through his ears. He called it the 'Triple Filter Test.'

Three Filter Test: Truth, Goodness, Usefulness

Once Socrates was going somewhere, and a learned friend of his beckoned him from behind. He was eager to say something to Socrates. He said I want to tell you something about your friend.

Socrates stopped him midway. He said I have a policy only to hear those things that pass the triple filter test.

The friend had no idea about this triple filter said, but he knew Socrates to be a little quirky. He wanted to know about this test.

Socrates explained that he'd only hear it if you can vouch that whatever you will tell me will pass any of the three parameters.

Truth: The first parameter is of truth.

- Are you certain that whatever you are going to tell me is true?
- Have you seen it happen?
- Do you have any means to be sure that it is true?

The friend said that he had heard it from a reliable, but had no means to ensure that it was true.

Socrates said, never mind. We'll now judge it on the second scale—the scale of goodness.

Goodness: Socrates said, whatever you are about to tell me

- Will it be something good about my friend?
- Would it tell me something positive?

The friend was getting impatient now, but he had to admit that it wouldn't add anything good about his friend. But, On the contrary, it might be defaming.

Socrates stopped him midway. He said that you would tell me something about my friend, which is neither good nor you have any means to be sure that it is true. Yet you want me to hear it.

Anyway, there is still the last filter left. If the information passes the test, you can still tell me.

Usefulness: Socrates wanted to know whether the information would be useful for him in any way.

- Would this information add value to my life and knowledge?
- Will it make me happy?
- Will it be beneficial for me?

The friend said that the information wasn't going to do any of that.

Socrates told him that in that case, he wouldn't want to hear that gossip.

However, the story doesn't end here. You'd want to hear more of it.

That person wanted to tell Socrates that one of his dear friends was having an affair with his wife. There was no way he could be certain about it. He had also heard it from someone. But, he felt that this news should be told to Socrates.

Did he have good intentions behind it?

There is no way we could tell that now. However, we know one thing for sure that Socrates dodged a bullet that day.

If Socrates had allowed this person to speak his mind, he would have told him about the affair.

Socrates, being Socrates, would have allotted a lot of time and energy thinking about it. The news would have enraged him and made him question a few things in life. He might have lost a wife and a friend that day. Yet, he couldn't have done anything to reverse the fact that his friend was having an affair with his wife. What made things worse, there was no way to know whether the news was true.

The moral of the story is that you can allow all sorts of information to pollute your mind without knowing their usefulness, credibility, or intent. Propaganda, vested interests, and a will to somehow influence others' opinions are the main objective of most corporates, media houses, news agencies, opinion-makers, and political parties.

If you allow unfiltered access, you'll have more and more mental clutter. Therefore, careful analysis of whatever you are absorbing is very important.

Use Your Mind Consciously

We can do very little about the information we have been consuming since our childhood. It is already etched in our memory. However, if we are aware and mindful, we can prevent further accumulation of mental clutter. Mindfulness can also help you in preventing your thoughts from clouding your judgment.

Mindfulness is a simple way of living that can help you become conscious of the information you grasp and your actions. It is not some technique that you need to learn in a class. It is a way of life that you'd need to practice wholeheartedly.

In the chapters ahead, we will try to understand and practice mindfulness in greater detail. We will also discuss how it can help you reduce mental clutter and unremitting mind chatter.

Mindfulness may seem to be a very heavy word indicating something complex. On the contrary, it is the process of simplifying life. Mindfulness is the way towards shunning the life running on the autopilot and taking active charge of it.

Our lives have become monotonous, uneventful, and robotic. You can't deny that most of the things you do in the day are out of habit.

We eat every day. We keep longing to eat better. We want tastier food. We want a better ambiance. We want better service—newer items on the menu.

However,

- Can you recall the last time you had paid attention to the food you have so many demands?
- Can you recall the last time when you had paid complete attention to the food you were eating and could feel every ingredient used in it?
- Can you recall the last time you had enjoyed the food for its taste, smell, freshness, texture, and other genuine qualities?

Most of us wouldn't be able to remember such a moment. Now, I'd like you to remember a favorite dish of your childhood. I can assure you that even today, you'll be able to feel its taste in your mouth.

How does that happen?

As kids, our minds are uncluttered. We can pay attention to things. Kids may look distracted, hyperactive, and lost in their games, but because their minds are not cluttered, retaining even such minor details is easy.

As an adult, even while you are sitting in the swankiest diner, you are thinking a thousand things. Even if you think about that place and its food, your mind is always wandering about associated things. You are trying to judge the service of the server. You want bang for your buck, and hence your mind is focused on the ambiance, the people around, the decoration, and the bragging rights it'll give you. Most of the time, you may even remain occupied in taking selfies of the food or the place.

The food will always come secondary because it was never on the priority list. It is one of the biggest issues with mindlessness. We lose our priorities as well as our objectives. We keep on wandering here and there. We give importance to things that do not mean anything. We assume importance.

You must have heard about people committing suicides or going into depression over their social media posts getting disliked or not getting enough likes. For any sane person, it should be preposterous. But in this day and age, it is becoming the new normal.

Random things are driving us. We have started emphasizing things because some celebrity or influencer is promoting the same. We do not use due diligence. We do not take into account that all those people have their vested interests behind promoting something.

Mindfulness is a way to put a stop to this madness of mindless activity.

Mindfulness requires you to pay attention to every minute detail in life. You stop giving attention to one part and discarding the other.

When you eat, you only eat. You pay attention to every part of the food in front of you. You don't judge it or compare it with others. You only try to feel every aspect of the food in front of you.

Feeling the taste, smell, texture, and enjoying it to the fullest is the mindfulness. You do not push the food down your throat while fiddling with your phone, watching TV, or talking to your friends. Mindful eating means paying complete attention to the food you are eating. Enjoying every morsel of food you take. Feel its taste and texture while you chew it ample times. You give the respect that food deserves.

Mindfulness is a practice you can follow in every aspect of life. You can think mindfully, eat mindfully, walk mindfully, work mindfully, and live mindfully. It is a way of life that can help you take active charge of your mind and body.

When you are watching TV or doing something else while eating, you allow your subconscious to take charge.

You stop paying attention to the task that you should, and you begin absorbing information that you shouldn't.

Mindfulness is the way to become sincere in life. You learn to take things one at a time. It doesn't mean being slow. It only means being efficient and effective in the use of available resources. It is one of the best ways to cut down mental clutter.

When your mind is not wandering in different directions, the power of observation increases immensely. You can think, see, and act with greater clarity.

If you are mindful, you will be able to control your thoughts actively. The clutter in your mind would thin out, and mind chatter would have no impact on your functioning.

We will learn how to incorporate mindfulness in life and understand how it will help you deal with mental clutter.

Chapter 7: What Does Decluttering the Thoughts Mean?

Decluttering is a very simple term. It means organizing things. It means putting things in order. It means indexing or labeling things so they can be easily retrieved when they are needed.

I purposefully focused on words like organizing, indexing, labeling, and putting things in order because, unlike physical clutter, mental clutter can't always be thrown out or dumped.

We always try to let go of the past and memories' baggage that only impediments clear thinking. But we seldom succeed. It is not always possible to drive out every bad thought that you have in mind. Some memories are entrenched very deep, and they are bad only in parts and have some wonderful things attached to them.

There are thought essential patterns. You can't just throw them out.

Some thoughts and memories are dispensable. You will do much better without them. Although driving out even those memories isn't easy, yet it is possible. It is always best to let them slip past into oblivion.

Decluttering of thought means identification and labeling of thoughts. You do not let every thought in your mind have its equal influence on your functioning. You stop providing unhindered access to every thought.

You classify thoughts as useful and useless. Once you have classified the thoughts, you become mindful of those thoughts.

Being mindful about your thoughts empowers you to stop any useless thought from affecting the conscience.

However, that is the later stage that you must intend to achieve.

You begin the process of decluttering by understanding the thoughts. You will have to pay attention to the thoughts and the way they form.

Meditation and detachment are the ways that can help you in this process.

Meditation is a very powerful and effective way to help you unravel the mind. It gives you the power to look within and become aware.

It opens the path of consciousness for you.

Meditation is the simple technique of looking within yourself with your awareness as the medium. It helps you search within. All the puzzles that you've been trying to solve outside can be solved by closing your mind. Meditation is the tool for that.

It is the path of Buddha.

Meditation helps you relax your mind and calm down your thoughts. It brings clarity about the thoughts that are creating fear and anxiety patterns in the mind. It can help you remain unaffected while they are doing their thing.

It helps you classify thoughts as useful and useless and only allow useful thoughts to have a role in your thinking process.

Meditation- The Path to Detachment from the Mental Clutter

Most people feel enraged and crushed that the incessant mental chatter in their minds makes their lives miserable. They are always having so many thoughts about trivial issues that they find it hard to focus on anything. Negative thoughts keep bombarding their thought process, making normal functioning increasingly difficult for them.

These are the people who wish they could stop their minds even for a bit to relax.

Unfortunately, stopping the thoughts from originating and flowing is not possible. As we have already discussed, the mind will go on doing its thing. However, mind having thoughts is not your problem. Your problem is that your mind is only having bad thoughts. You identify with those thoughts, and that's why they have such a powerful dominance over them.

Let us consider the analogy of traffic.

Suppose you have just returned from a meeting, and you are standing in the balcony of your hotel room. You've called it a day, and it was a productive day indeed.

You have accomplished the task, and you are pleased with the result. You are standing relaxed in the balcony with your favorite beverage in hand.

There is no tussle in your mind.

You are looking at the busy road ahead of you. There is a traffic jam. It is massive. Cars are stuck on the road. People are honking desperately. They are ready to fight. But they are far away.

You can't hear the honking or shouting. You are just looking and imagining the mood.

The traffic doesn't bother you a bit. You don't feel the rush. You don't feel the anger. It is just another seen flashing in front of your eyes.

Now, let us flip this scene over.

Imagine going back from your office to your home. Some guests are waiting at your home. You have groceries to pick en route. You have a long line of cars ahead of you and a longer one behind you.

Can you feel the anger and anguish now?

It is the same traffic. But earlier, it was not affecting you. Not because it was any less intense, but because you were not identifying with it. Now you are in that traffic. Some people can still stay calm in that traffic. They know that it will ease out on its own. They need not put any effort into it. They know their efforts will be futile. They know the value of detachment.

Our mental chatter is also the same.

Our mind produces thousands of thoughts a day. It is a continuous process. If we begin paying attention to every thought, we will have no energy left to pay attention to real-life things.

If you learn to identify useful and useless thoughts, you'll not need to bother about the negative ones.

It can be achieved through meditation and mindfulness.

Meditation helps you in understanding and classifying your thoughts. Mindfulness helps you in only giving those thoughts priority that needs one. It is the process of gaining control over your active mind.

Most people think that meditation is a difficult process. Getting hold of the mind is difficult. You are unable to sit for a moment without thought; sitting in a thoughtless state for longer than that would be impossible.

It needs a lot of practice, dedication, and time.

There is no basis to the point that meditation is a difficult process. Our mind is our most important companion. It is always active and with you all the time. Hence you do not need to fear the mind.

People have a misconception that meditation is about thoughtlessness. They have a prejudice against the thought. Meditation is not about thoughtlessness but conscious thinking. When you meditate, you get the power to look into your mind with your awareness and invigilate those thoughts. It empowers you to make useless thoughts ineffective. Therefore, you do not need to sit in a state of thoughtlessness. You simply need to be aware and conscious.

The other part is that meditation needs a lot of practice, dedication, and time. It is a fact. There is no way you can hold any power over your thoughts and mind if you are not ready to practice or devote some time to it. Your current state of mind is a result of negligence, and you can see the result.

Therefore, you'll have to practice meditation and devote some time to it. But you do not need to worry as you are already wasting a lot more time than that in a state of confusion, panic, and frustration.

Meditation is not something that you'll need to go somewhere to learn. You'll need to practice, but you can do that anytime, anywhere. People forget that meditation and mindfulness are ways of life.

You do not need specific settings to be mindful and meditative. To look inside your mind, you only need to be prepared.

Guided Meditation Practice For Bringing Awareness of Thoughts

We will now practice a simple meditation to become aware of thoughts. It is a simple exercise into self-awareness. You need to look closely into your thought and try to find what's inside them that scares or troubles you.

You can record this meditation script in your voice and use it as a guided meditation to help you through the process. It'll help you understand that meditation is not a difficult process, but an amazingly powerful one. It can help you relax completely and calm your thoughts.

Preparation

Please take a seat
Become comfortable
Let your body and mind relax completely
Initially, anything and everything may become a distraction
You do not need to bother
Those are temporary distractions
It is preferable to wear loose-fitting, comfortable clothes

Initially, when you sit for meditation
Your mind may wander here and there
Several thoughts may come swarming
No matter how hard you try to resist
It'll still happen
Please do not pay attention to it
However, it is always a good idea to sit with a pen and paper
In the initial few minutes while you are relaxing
If anything important crosses your mind
Write that down on paper
Do not try to store it in your mind as it'll keep coming back
Such thoughts cause the greatest distraction

Use a comfortable cushion for sitting
Uncomfortable seating position can keep drawing your attention
For meditation, the full lotus position is usually the best

However, it can be difficult for many people
Try to sit normally in a cross-legged position

During the meditation session
You'll need to keep your back upright
If you slouch, you may feel lazy or distracted
If you want, you can use a backrest

Please keep your neck straight
But, never use a neck rest
Also, keep your chin raised a little

Please sit straight but do not make your body stiff
Keep your shoulders parallel to each other
You can keep your hand on your knees or even in your lap
Keep your palms facing upwards
Ensure that there is no physical stress
Make adjustments of position by leaning forward and sideways a few times

(Now give yourself a few minutes to relax. Do not rush this time. Use this time to calm the mind or to allow your thoughts to settle. If you have anything specific in your mind, write it down.)

Initiation

Please ensure that you are comfortable and relax
Now, close your eyes gently
There is no reason to think anything

Close your eyes and relax

Do not feel stressed
You do not need to do anything
You do not need any preparation
You only need to relax

Do not bother about the procedure
Do not bother about the duration
Relax completely
You do not even need to control your mind

Focus your awareness on your breathing
Feel the breath coming in
Feel the breath going out

Inhale
Exhale

Inhale
Exhale

Inhale
Exhale

Allow your breathing to become normal
Let it regain its rhythmic pace
It will have its music
When your breathing is natural
Your mind is calm
You can hear the faintest noises

Keep your awareness focused on the process of breathing
Do not think of other things
You do not need to manage your breathing
There is no need for control
Only observe the breathing

Breathe in
Breathe out

Breathe in
Breathe out

Breathe in

Breathe out

(Long)

Breathing is calm now
It is stable and smooth
There is no rush
There is no fear

We'll now do deep breathing
We'll inhale slowly but deeply through the nostrils
We will try to fill up as much air as we can
Then, we will hold that air for a bit
Finally, release all that air even more slowly through the mouth

This deep breathing exercise helps us calm the mind
It will drive away negative thoughts
It will increase the focus

While you inhale
Please keep your awareness glued to your breathing
Observe the way your body behaves
See the way your chest, belly, and lungs inflate
Feel the pressure that builds during the process
And most importantly, feel the relief you get when you release the breath through your mouth
Though your awareness, observe everything

You may have some thoughts
They may distract you
They may draw your awareness initially
Do not resist or ignore those thoughts
Observe those thoughts
Acknowledge them
But, bring your awareness back to your breathing
There is nothing more than this breathing

Let us begin by inhaling through the nostrils
Keep breathing in
Let your pace be steady
There is no need to rush
As you begin inhaling
You'll feel your chest expand
Fill up your lungs with fresh air
You'll see your belly expand rapidly
Fill up all the air you can
Keep breathing in until you can't
When you know, you are full
You have to wait

Remain calm
You'll feel the mounting pressure
It is the moment when you can scan your whole brain in moments
There will be no fears or temptations
Your awareness has all the control
You might feel a little uncomfortable
Please hold the breath as long as you can
You will hear the rhythmic 'thud' of the heart even louder
The pressure will become unbearable

Breathe out through your mouth
You will need to be even slower
There should be control
Do not rush
Roll your lips and allow the air to exit slowly
At first, all the excess air will go out
But, you are not finished
You need to push out all the air
Please push your belly towards your back
Empty all the spent air inside you
Keep pushing until you can't

Now, Relax!

Feel the wave of relaxation take over you
You'll feel calmer and relaxed

Allow your breathing to become normal
Breathe in
Breathe out

Breathe in
Breathe out

Breathe in
Breathe out

Now, bring your awareness to your thoughts
We will explore the thoughts
Observe them from close quarters

Your thoughts and your awareness are not the same
They are two distinct entities
Your thoughts are subjective
They are based on your memories and experiences
They draw inspiration from your fears and insecurities
They can be joyful, sad, fearful, horrifying
They can vary in intensity
Your current mental state will affect your thoughts
Your mood will empower them

Your awareness is objective
It is analytical
It will always be neutral
It is devoid of emotions
It is logical but calm

Your subconscious mind drives your thoughts
Awareness comes from the active mind

At the moment, you are awake
Your awareness will help you separate facts from memories
You have the power to discern real from unreal

Observe the thoughts forming in your mind
The doubt that is building up
The fear that looks real but isn't
You can see all of it with the help of your awareness

Observe the way thoughts form in your mind
How they mature
Take references from your memories
Influence your thinking
Then go away

Thoughts are not permanent
They have a short life-span
But your awareness is always with you
It is always the same
It is a skill that you'll need to explore
The more you dig into your awareness
The sharper and more powerful it'll get

The restlessness, the anxiety, and the fear you feel
All come from these thoughts
But, your thoughts are not permanent
They come and go
They are powerless
You can discard everything with your awareness
But, if your awareness is weak
If you do not have active control
These thoughts will prevail

Most people live with the thought that everything is futile
They see no meaning in life
They feel that they are a cog in the wheel
They have no active role
They have no significance
They feel that they are unfortunate
They lack the things others have
They lack the opportunities others have
Mental clutter does that to you

Our failures in life
Missed opportunities
Lack of initiatives
Make us feel so
These are just feelings
They have no real meaning
They are baseless fears

The more you rely on your thoughts
The higher will be the negativity
All this is not real
It is your imagination forcing you to remain in a shell

Focus your awareness at the center of your forehead
Focus on that point
You are not looking for something
You may see some light ebbing from that point
Keep your awareness glued to it

Do you know?
A Quarter million people would have died last night
These many people die every day
They will not see the light of the day
You are not among them
Is that not a thing to be happy?
Did you smile in the morning when you woke up?
Smile that you are alive
You are not among the unfortunate ones to have passed away

Every person has loved ones
The people who care for that person
The people who feel about that person
Let us assume that every person has five to ten people in life who care
This morning would have had a bad start for at least two and a half million people at least
They would have lost someone dear to them
If you are not among the people who have lost someone dear today
Is it not something to be happy about?
Aren't you fortunate that you are not among them?

Our thoughts make us see what's bad around us
It is only our awareness that can wake up to the good
It can fill you with optimism
It can help you leave the past behind and live in the present

How to Declutter Your Mind

You do not need to fear your thoughts
You only need to be more aware and awake
Do not live in fear of life
Embrace this life
You can only find joy when you begin to live this life fully

Bring your awareness to your breathing

Breathe in
Breathe out

Breathe in
Breathe out

Breathe in
Breathe out

Allow your breathing to become normal
Let it regain its natural pace
Keep breathing normally

Now, become aware of your senses
With your eyes still closed
Try to feel your surrounding
Listen if there are noises in the background
Try to sense the smells around you
Feel the sensations on your skin

Please do not open your eyes yet
Try to move your fingers a little
Now, try to move your toes

Give your shoulders a roll
You can now open your eyes gently

Please do not try to get up all of a sudden
Enjoy the calm of the mind for a bit
Focus on your awareness

When you are ready
Please get up slowly

Thank You!

Chapter 8: What Are You Missing While Working With A Cluttered Mind?

A cluttered mind is ill-equipped to work. With the increase in the mental clutter, the anxiety levels and sleep irregularities begin escalating. You may also face difficulties in paying attention to important things as your attention span reduces drastically. Hyperactivity and juggling between chores may become your second nature.

A cluttered mind is effectively less productive as there is no focus and dedication to the task. It will propel you to look for coping mechanisms. Complete avoidance of the problems becomes their primary objective.

The more clutter you have, the serious the problem gets. You may feel none of it in the beginning, but slowly these changes begin to take effect.

Most of all, a cluttered mind can make you miss some of the basic but most important aspects of life. Sorting of mental clutter will have a much wider impact on your mind and your life as a whole.

Some of the most important changes that you might experience are:

Freedom From Anxiety, Stress, and Lack of Focus: Clutter brings stress. Irrespective of the fact whether the clutter is physical or mental, it is going to bring stress. The more clutter you have around you, the higher the mental engagement, slower response time, and lower focus. Less is more when it comes to clutter. The researchers at Princeton University Neuroscience Institute found that the clutter present in your visual field also competes for neural representation. It means that the higher the number of things in your surrounding, the lower your ability to focus on a specific thing. The clutter would keep drawing your attention through various mediums.

It isn't very different, even in the case of mental clutter. The greater the mental clutter, the difficult it gets for you to focus on anything.

The clutter is irritating, and it may lead to frustration. If you fear something or have any phobia, your mind will keep playing that in a loop. No matter how harder you try to push it out, it will stick.

It is the reason stress and anxiety become a common feature in the lives of cluttered people.

Not addressing the clutter in your mind is a choice. You can choose not to do anything. However, it will keep you trapped with the same fears, anxieties, and insecurities.

UCLA researchers have found a correlation between clutter and the main stress hormone 'Cortisol.' If there is excess clutter in and around you, your life is bound to remain tough.

Decluttering the mind is the easy way out of most mental issues. A very important thing that most people are unaware of is that clutter of any sort is inciting a response.

If you have mental clutter, the thoughts are trying to provoke you to take some action to address them. There are two options in front of you. First, you can choose to face the issue and end it once and for all. It is the fight response. Second, you can choose to dodge the bullet and evade it. It is the flight response. Although you didn't take any physical action, your mind was continuously making difficult decisions. It was engaged. It was distracted. If the clutter is high, your mind will be forced to take such flight and fight decisions again and again. It will raise your cortisol levels for sure.

Therefore, the increased stress and anxiety levels are a psychological change and a physiological change. Your mind is constantly dealing with decision fatigue, and that is not going to be helpful anyway.

Decluttering your mind can help you experience freedom from consistent decision fatigue. Perpetual decision fatigue that you have been experiencing. Stress and anxiety emanating from cluttered thoughts would cease to exist. You will get better control of your thoughts and would be able to make rational decisions.

Clarity of Thought: Muddling of thoughts is another malice that people with decluttered mind constantly face. They have no clarity of thought because they are unable to rationalize with the current situation. They are always thinking about too many things at the same time. In their minds, they feel as if they are thinking in future terms where they are trying to analyze any action's pros and cons. In reality, their mind is only trying to find a way to evade the situation. It is looking for an escape route so that any escalation can be prevented. It is not only true to aggressive events but even for the events that require simple decision-making. They fear deciding because they don't want to be held responsible for them.

Poor clarity of thought is a big disadvantage of mental clutter. It makes you very defensive and makes you analyze so many things at the same time that there can be no outcome. You try to look for similar actions in the past and their outcomes and base your current actions on them. When you do not find exact reference matches, you feel even more confused.

When you have a decluttered mind, you are free to evaluate things on their merit. You are not looking for references from the past but base your decisions on the current scenarios. Therefore, fear, greed, favor, anticipation, and other such emotional factors have no role in your decisions.

When your mind is free of clutter, you can look at things with complete clarity. There is coordination between your thoughts and actions.

End of Procrastination: Mental clutter generates many 'should's' and 'could's.' You are always trying to figure out the best way to do a thing and always feel stuck. There is no end to the list of things that get delayed due to procrastination. When you are full of mental clutter, you are never able to figure out the best approach.

Napoleon used to say, 'I may lose a war, but I will never lose a minute.' The day he wasted time thinking, it turned out to be his Waterloo.

Procrastination makes you lose minutes, hours, days, months, and years. There is no action but postponement.

It all happens because there is no clarity of thought. Even small tasks keep getting delayed. In the end, even those minor tasks become unmanageable.

Freedom from mental clutter helps you become clear about your immediate and future goals. It makes you set specific deadlines so that you have ample time to take action.

Ability to 'Live in the Moment': Most people with clutter are living in their minds. They are fearful of everything wrong that has happened in the past, and they are sure that something worse will happen in the future.

Therefore, they live in fear of the past and future, and both are in their minds. This fear is crippling. It leads to inaction. They are never able to come out of their protective bubble.

The life is in the present. What has happened is in the past. It can't affect you today. The future is yet to come, and hence there is nothing to fear from it if you work in the present.

However, mental clutter makes them lose perspective. People surrender to their fears and stop taking any action.

Decluttering the mind helps you in living in the moment. It gives you an understanding that whatever you have is in the present. Life is very uncertain. We may plan for years and decades, but we are not sure of the next moment. Whatever you do, your action in the present will determine your future, and hence wasting this moment is illogical.

When you begin to live in the present, achieving anything becomes a possibility. You are capable of enjoying the moment on its merit.

Continued Growth: Decluttering the mind is a way to ensure that you are not fearful of the opportunities and challenges. It allows you to weigh everything on its merits and hence continued growth, irrespective of the challenges, always remains in perspective.

If you do not want your growth to be stalled by minor events in life and grow evenly, getting freedom from clutter should be your prime objective.

Humankind has a unique gift of intelligence. We are a thinking race. We can imagine and plan things. These are very powerful abilities. However, clutter can make these abilities work against us.

It makes our imagination work against us and also brings procrastination in the name of planning.

Decluttering of the mind helps get rid of all these issues, and you can grow to your full potential.

Chapter 9: Is Decluttering Really Effective and Possible?

It is a pertinent question that will arise in your mind.

Decluttering is not an easy process. You can also be sure that shortcuts don't work in this process. Therefore, it is natural for you to worry about the results.

The short and satisfying answer to this question is that decluttering the mind is possible and effective. It will yield all the results that have been discussed in the book and many more.

However, while this answer is true, it is not complete.

While decluttering the mind is possible, it is not one act that can be completed in exclusion. While you are trying to declutter your mind, you will also need to declutter your physical surroundings, leading to clutter.

The same goes for relationships clutter as well as clutter at your workplace.

You will also have to work on your responsibilities and priorities in life. Ignoring information overload through social media platforms and the internet will also not be wise, and we will have to clear that too.

Decluttering the mind is a wholesome act where work in all the quarters of life is reflected in mental clarity.

Some people wrongly believe that if they meditate daily for a while and do some exercises, they can keep mental clutter away. It is a very limited approach. While meditation can help them keep mental chatter calm, it is never a permanent solution.

When you are not meditating, your mind is getting the same fodder it was getting earlier, and hence it will work the same way.

Decluttering the mind involves getting rid of all the things that have been holding you back. It would involve your fears, insecurities, and aspirations that you know you can't meet.

Decluttering the mind means eliminating the should have's and could have's' from life. You can't stick to what you could have done but didn't or what you should have done, but you didn't.

It is an approach of looking for the most important things in life and letting go of all the unhelpful activities.

Most importantly, decluttering is looking for the things that matter the most.

If you are determined and disciplined, decluttering is a simple and effective process.

Important Parts of the Decluttering Process

Brake the Chains

Have you ever give it a thought that your mind and your habits are the biggest barriers to your happiness. You keep piling up small tasks and never feel truly liberated. Your mind is always worried about those tasks, but you keep putting off those tasks for later.

What do you do with the time that you save?

You worry about those tasks.

You can never feel truly free until you have those tasks at the back of your mind. You'll keep thinking about them and worry.

Such tasks are true obstacles. They'll drain you and create a severe imbalance in your life. With every passing day, the weight would increase, and even if you haven't done anything the previous day, you'll wake up feeling burned out.

It doesn't happen by chance. It is a routine when you are procrastinating by habit. Physically you may not be doing the task, but your mind is always worrying about them.

Those can be small personal chores pending for long or even professional tasks that you have been putting off. These will ruin your productivity and steal your mental balance. Unknowingly, your mind will always keep thinking about them.

It can be a simple task of saying sorry to your partner of applying for a new job. No matter the nature of the task, it will occupy your mind and create clutter if it is pending. It will keep you tied down. You will remain shackled.

The first thing you need to do is break the barriers in your mind. It would help if you cleared your mental backlogs before beginning to declutter other aspects of life.

Procrastination is of the biggest causes of mental clutter. It also leads to fear, guilt, resentment, and other such negative feelings. If you stop procrastinating, you'll have more time to manage your tasks and schedules.

It will make you feel more energetic and rejuvenated. You will not get distracted by small tasks, as you would have taken care of them as they arose. It doesn't take a lot to do small tasks. The only thing you need is the will. If you begin clearing smaller tasks instantly, you'll realize that you have more time and energy to spare for bigger objectives. The mental clutter on your mind will also reduce.

People with a decluttered mind feel dread when they feel that they have a new task assigned. They do not know the way to accommodate those tasks. It happens because nothing is organized in their lives. They have been postponing so many things for the future that their future has no scope for anything new.

Such people can't feel excited about anything new. They lose the feeling of joy even in those things that are valuable for them. They have no joy and peace in their personal lives. Their personal space is also filled with worries that have transcended the boundaries of work.

- Cutting this clutter should be your primary and most important task
- You can't do that all at once. You must begin by finishing the simplest of tasks first
- Handle everything that keeps coming your way
- Do not put off tasks for later, even if they are insignificant or may not cause big trouble in the future. Clutter may even win by sheer number. The higher the number of pending tasks, the greater the clutter.

Think It Through But Never Overthink

Are you allowing day-dreaming to become a euphemism for your habit of overthinking?

Do you find it hard to sleep at night because several thoughts come rushing to you?

It is a fact that a cluttered mind has a lot to think about. The thoughts are the fodder for a cluttered mind.

But, have you ever thought about the things you are thinking?

The thoughts are muddled, and there is never a focus on specific things. The mind keeps jumping from one thought to another.

Let us take a popular example of Youtube. It is a popular video streaming website that most of us use. When you go to Youtube, are you always able to stick to the things you wanted to see?

It never happens. You open one video, but then you see another interesting suggestion, and there is a temptation. One video leads to another, and by the time you think of closing it, you are watching something completely different from what you initially intended.

Our mind also works similarly. It pushes you towards one thought, and before you can conclude, it jumps to another.

Your thoughts keep rotating, and other aspects like imagination, assumption, fears, and anxieties jump in.

You driving your thoughts is a good thing, but your thoughts driving you can be a disaster in the making.

Meditation and mindfulness are the two very important processes that can help you deal with such circling thoughts. Mindfulness can help you understand the futility of thoughts, making you spin in circles.

It would be best if you thought things through. It is a very important aspect of being human. However, getting caught in the spiral of overthinking can be self-sabotaging.

Cultivate Calm Around Yourself

It is one of the easiest things to do. Clearing physical clutter is easy. You might feel a pinch initially, but there will be no looking back once you begin feeling lighter.

Most of us do not realize that physical clutter around us has a deep impact on our mental clutter. It keeps our mind overstimulated and diverts our focus.

Adopting a minimalist approach in life is always the best as it helps in preventing clutter.

Reducing physical clutter is only one step towards minimalism. It lowers the decision-fatigue you feel every day. You do not have to make choices frequently because there are limited, only very useful things around.

Once you get habitual of employing minimalism physically, you'd find it much easier to use it in your personal and professional life.

Let go of the things that are draining you mentally, emotionally, or financially. We all have such things in plenty. We have many toxic relationships that we can't sustain. Yet, we cling on to them with the hope that they'll improve. Such a time never comes.

Several incidents in the past have a deep impact on us emotionally. We know they are holding us back, but we still never allow them to take a back seat.

There are white elephants in our possession that are nothing more than a financial drain. We know our inability to sustain then, yet we can never muster the courage to wash our hands of those things.

These decisions are never easy but must be taken for the larger good. You can never completely declutter your life until you have identified such things and eliminated them.

It is never an easy decision but important, nevertheless.

The key to success is to move one step at a time. Take baby steps into any change and acclimatize yourself to the change. If you try to make too many drastic changes simultaneously, sustaining them for long can become difficult.

Sustainability in your routine, personal, and professional life is a very important criterion for success.

Decluttering physical, personal, and professional space may seem like cutting down on many things. However, that is not the correct perspective. When you eliminate a few things, you have more time and attention to give to others. The important aspects that have been getting neglected until now will begin to get the attention they always deserved.

When this happens, you'll experience the calm that you have always been yearning for. You'd have better focus, and you'll be able to enjoy life with greater enthusiasm.

It takes away a big load from your shoulders and makes you feel more content and alive.

Set Your Priorities Right

Wrong priorities are painful and cluttering. Most of the time, we are unaware of the things we really want from our lives. We begin setting goals because even others have done the same.

We choose incorrect career paths and then keep sulking for the rest of our lives. We set incorrect standards of happiness and then brood about being unhappy. We have wrong or unrealistic expectations from our loved ones and then keep complaining about incompatibility.

As you can see, there is one main culprit in all these issues. We are the culprit. There is no way we can manage others. We are never able to come to terms with the fact that others are also individuals with different aspirations, aims, and expectations. They can, at the most, adjust but never completely transform.

The incorrect choices and expectations we have with ourselves are the most difficult to deal with because we have no one to blame for them.

Real transformation can only happen when you set your priorities right.

You will have to understand what makes you happy. You will have to forget what the world would think about it. You will have to ignore the standards set by society or your peers. Until you do that, happiness will always elude you, and guilt and regret will remain your companion.

Correct identification of the things that give you true happiness is very important.

You must realize that this is one life that you have for living. There is nothing beyond and above this life.

Our lives are like ticking time bombs. There is a fixed time. It is ticking uninterrupted. No matter what you do in your life, you cannot win even one extra second of life. It is the most precious possession you have.

It is always your choice to waste it in pursuits that you think others will appreciate or take positive measures to make it worthwhile.

With this life, we make a lot of difference in the lives of others around us. This difference can be positive or negative as they make in ours. You have a choice whether you want to use this opportunity or waste this resource.

If you want to make a positive difference in others' lives, you will have to make your life positive. Until you are exuberant with life, you can't do anything for others.

If you want to declutter your mind, you will have to identify one prime goal and more towards it with focus. Everything else should be secondary, as all paths lead to the same destination.

Chapter 10: The Efficiency of Decluttering Depends on 3 Important Things

As I have amply stressed, decluttering the mind is a lengthy process. There can be no two views about it. There are no shortcuts, and if there are, they'll not work.

While decluttering the mind, your main adversary is your mind. You have a powerful adversary, and you must always respect your opponent.

The evolution of the human mind is a work of millions of years. Your fears, insecurities, anxieties, and stress mechanism all have distinct functions. Nothing is wasteful.

The problems you are facing are not the problems of the mind but your own making. We all are born like a clean slate. Most of our habits, fears, and inhibitions are acquired. It is the already present mechanism in mind that gives them such a spin.

The mind is designed to follow the thought process that you pick. You always have a choice, and you apparently picked a wrong path to walk.

However, our mind is malleable. It is an ever-young organ. Our brain never gets old and frail, although our body does. It was the reason the wisdom of older men has always been trusted so much. Our brain cells die and then regenerate. The brain remains young forever if you are providing it the right nutrition.

The problem with toxic thoughts and clutter is that they are poisoning the mind. They are making our brains incapable of productivity. They are pushing so much useless fodder in the form of clutter that the mind loses its power of discernment. It develops a negative thought pattern. It forgets the dangers of assuming things and making deductions based on them.

There are three important principles for helping the mind regain its efficiency.

Process

Our mind works in a pattern. Every individual has a way of thinking. However, that way is picked. We choose the way we will think. There is a heavy influence from the environment we grow in. Our peers also have a role in it in the growing years.

Hence, there is no way you can change the way you think overnight. It will need awareness, mindfulness, and process.

If you want to declutter your mind, you will have to pick a process you want to run. A mind with positive thinking doesn't develop out of the blue. It takes a lot of conditioning and preparation.

Negative thoughts originate in mind because you have been thinking pessimistically. Being critical of things or about yourself is a good thing if that is done to improve. But, when it turns into self-pity, you begin to sink deep very fast.

You hear voices in your head all the time about the dangers of doing anything. You fear before taking any action. You begin to find your comfort zone and fear coming out of it. Everything in life becomes telling you about the wrong things about to happen.

Such a negative bias can be very dangerous. It can keep you trapped inside your mind. Your mind would begin to warn you against taking any action as it can be dangerous. You would begin to ruminate over everything to make certain that it is safe. It never is.

Negative thought patterns are very dangerous, and they need to be broken.

> **Awareness:** Your awareness is a formidable weapon that can help you break these negative thought patterns. Your subconscious mind would keep pushing fearful thoughts and project negative outcomes as a reality. Your awareness can help you discern them and realize that they are just thought. It has the

power to analyze facts and deduce the risk involved. You will have to become more aware of your thoughts. Whenever such thoughts or doubts arise about anything, you must use your intellect or awareness to look deep within those insecurities.

Labeling of Thoughts: As we have discussed, our mind is a big warehouse where you can park unlimited data, but it is not an efficient one. It doesn't distinguish between a product or destructive thought. The survival instinct in our brain is more likely to pick negative thoughts to ensure better protection. However, we do not need this shield all the time. At least, not in these times when we are comparatively safer and secure. Your mind will keep throwing thoughts at you; it is the job of your awareness to label these thoughts as 'helpful' or 'unhelpful.' Once you label a thought as unhelpful, it will lose its viciousness. It will also reassure you that your thoughts are not you. The feeling of control originates here.

Ask, Seek, Knock: Your mind is a perpetual thought machine. It will not stop. You cannot stop it. It should not be stopped. It only means that there is no way the mind would stop having all kinds of thoughts in so many words. However, you can ask your mind to stop as soon as it takes a negative track. If you feel that your mind is taking you on the wrong track, ask your mind loudly to stop. The thought is in your mind, and you can begin thinking about something else. But there are times when this is not possible. The thoughts are too powerful and disturbing. However, when you consciously ask your brain to stop loudly, it breaks the chain of thought for good.

Identify Your Triggers: We all have our Achilles heel. Some things make us feel more vulnerable than others. Such things are called triggers. They trigger the negative thought process. There can be specific people, situations, or even a physical state that may work as triggers. We all know the things that make us feel vulnerable. Avoidance is a strategy most people with mental clutter adopt, but they don't have proper identification of such triggers and the reasons behind those triggers. Living a life in fear is not an option if you want to live your life freely and positively. You must identify such triggers and understand the specific reasons behind your discomfort, uneasiness, and insecurities. Most triggers can be addressed. However, if specific triggers make you feel very uncomfortable and overcoming them is difficult, you can be selective about them. This approach shouldn't be generalized. You will have to be very specific about such things and narrow them down.

Practice

Practice makes us perfect, and it is very apt when it comes to our mind. Our mind is a slave of practice. Repetition of anything can help in perfecting it. Our behavior and reactions are nothing different.

Some kids are born left-handed. It is very natural. However, in certain parts of the world, doing certain things with the left hand is considered inauspicious or considered bad. For instance, in India's Hindu customs, eating from the left hand or performing religious acts using the left hand is frowned upon.

Parents begin instructing kids to do things by their right hands, and the mind picks it up. By the time they grow up, such kids begin using their right hand for all important tasks or become ambidextrous.

It is only one example of mind picking habits. It relies so much on practice that it can change the way limbs function. Changing the thought process is a little easier than that. You have your awareness by your side to guide and instruct your mind.

However, the most important thing here for changing the thought process is practice.

The way you think is not a one-time affair. It is your nature. We are talking about altering the whole pattern of thought. No trick can help you with this. You will only need practice.

Mindfulness is a way of life that helps you in living with your awareness. Living mindfully, you can inspect your thoughts and coordinate your thoughts and actions.

Our habits and thought process put us on autopilot mode. Almost 95 percent of the actions that we perform in our everyday lives are such actions that do not need our active interference. They happen because we are used to performing them in a certain way. Only 5 percent of actions need our active decision-making skills.

Let us begin with breathing. It is such a simple act. We do not need training for breathing. It is a natural process. Even in a vegetative state, a person will breathe. However, by modulating your breathing, you can alter your complete mental state.

If you are feeling agitated or anxious, a few deep breaths can calm you down. Even in the most aggressive state of mind, deep breathing for a few minutes can work wonders. Some people master the art of deep breathing and never feel agitated by anything.

Most of us know this, yet we can never think of breathing deep when feeling angry, anxious, or fearful, although it can help. The simple answer to this question is the lack of practice. In such a chaotic mental state, we lose our awareness because we are not in practice.

Mindfulness and Meditation are two magical ways to gain control of the mind, and you would need to practice these if you want to overcome mental clutter.

You will have to learn to remain conscious or aware of your thoughts and use your awareness to keep it calm.

Mindfulness is a magical way of life, but it will not come on its own. You will have to practice mindfulness in every walk of life.

Purpose

You cannot achieve any objective in life until there is an initiative for achieving it. The reward must always be desirable and tempting enough to keep you motivated.

Most people keep attending all the Ted-talks possible and watch countless motivational videos, but they can never sustain that fire for long. The reason is simple; they do not feel the objective rewarding enough. They have no purpose for which they should put in the amount of effort required.

Decluttering the mind isn't an easy task, but it is an important one.

However, you should know that no one has died of mental clutter. It isn't a physical ailment. It only makes life worthless enough to lose a sense of purpose.

Decluttering the mind can make your life easy, bring back your inner happiness, make you feel more relaxed and calm. You will find it easy to form stable and functioning relationships. Seamlessly navigating between personal and professional life would become possible for you.

You'll radiate positivity and would have a sense of purpose. You will not be spending life in this world but would be living it.

Although these are the goals for which many people would be willing to trade anything they might have, most people may not sacrifice what it takes to achieve the objective.

If you want to declutter your mind, you must have a clear purpose in your mind, and you must be determined to achieve it. The path of peace and tranquillity is not for those who do not have a sense of purpose or are not ready to become aware.

Peace and calm is not a reward enough for most people. They are always looking for something fancy. They want to have big adjectives attached to simple things, and these are the people who get disappointed mid-way.

> Gautama Buddha traveled thousands of miles on foot in search of enlightenment. He faced death many times in the forests. He was threatened by the kings and goons alike. For six years, he kept on trying everything possible to achieve enlightenment.
>
> He did rigorous fasting that nearly killed him. He punished his body so much that he almost died several times from the pain be had to bear. He was trying to find a way to attain knowledge.

People were amazed by the hardships of this prince sage. They believed that he could achieve something, and if they remained with him, even they would get that from him.

Finally, when Buddha lost all his hope of attaining enlightenment, he sat under a tree with the pledge that either he would get enlightenment or he would die trying.

Scriptures say that he sat under the Ficus tress for 49 days without moving from his place. He sat there without a single drop of water or food.

When he finally achieved enlightenment and opened his eyes, the disciples were eager to hear words of wisdom from him. He had a magical aura around him, and everyone was mystified.

However, Buddha said, I am hungry; let's cook some food.

The disciples were crestfallen. They could not believe their ears. They had no faith in him all of a sudden and looked at him like they were staring at a lunatic.

These were the same disciples who were ready to die with him in hunger. They had traveled thousands of miles. They had also borne all the discomfort and pain. Yet, they didn't expect to hear such words from a person who had achieved enlightenment just now.

Buddha achieved all that he achieved because he had a sense of purpose and he was determined. His disciples then couldn't achieve because they didn't have that sense of purpose, and they were only following for the sake of getting something.

A sense of purpose is one of the most important things required for eliminating clutter from your mind. Until you have a sense of purpose, you will not be able to push your mind to act against the patterns it has been following. A Poor sense of purpose can make you lax and careless.

Hence, a defined sense of purpose is the most important requirement for you to declutter and conquer your mind.

Chapter 11: Effective Ways to Declutter Your Mind

The human mind is insanely vast and immensely capable. It is capable of doing some of the most amazing things possible. Despite all the technological advancements made by medical science and technology, we are yet to uncover its capabilities to its full extent. However, we know that power works both ways. Power corrupts, and absolute power corrupts absolutely. A positive mind can help us achieve incredible feats, while a negative mind can lead to the destruction of the whole world.

The mind needs to be trained. It needs to be balanced. Human intellect is like a double-edged sword. It can work for and against us. If it isn't trained in the right direction, it will become anarchic. When you put too much power into something and don't give it a direction, there is every possibility that it will cause more destruction than betterment.

A cluttered mind is no different. It is full of confusion, and there is a lack of purpose. It is not going to be helpful for the individual who possesses it. Doubt, fear, anxieties, regrets, self-pity, resentment, and similar other emotions can become more powerful and begin to rule the individual.

Such an individual may cause more to oneself than others. It can make life difficult or uneasy. Even smaller goals may elude such person, and peace would remain a far-fetched thing.

However, the mind is malleable. It is never a lost cause like other things. No matter how cluttered a mind is, there is always a possibility to change the way a person things. There is always hope for a person trying to find calm in life.

Some of the common ways that can help you in calming your mind and decluttering its layers are:

Deep Breathing

Deep breathing is a surprisingly fast way to center your mind and get over the aggressive thoughts coming to your mind. We all try to remain calm and composed most of the time. However, there are still instances when keeping the mind in control can become difficult.

There are moments when our patience begins to run out, and the adrenaline rush begins kicking in. These are the moments of chaos when even the most composed people begin losing their grip of rationality and composure. The anger and frustration can be directed inwards or outwards, but the damage is serious irrespective of the direction.

At times, the mind is filled with fears and insecurities that can make you feel very vulnerable. There may not be a reason to fear, but the mind stops listening to reason. It makes the world a very insecure place for you at that moment.

Meditation and mindfulness are very powerful techniques to declutter the mind, but they are long-term measures. Such situations demand instant relief.

Deep breathing is a technique that can help you overcome all such scenarios irrespective of the place you are or the situation you are facing. It helps you calm the mind and get over the anxieties. It can calm a raging mind and pump some sense in a state of pumping fists.

The Process

Deep breathing is a very simple process. You do not need any preparation. You can practice deep breathing anytime, anywhere.

All of us breathe every moment of our lives. However, most of the time, our breathing is automatic. We are not monitoring it or supervising it. Our body and the mind do a fairly decent job of keeping us alive by coordinating our breathing as per need. When you are running, angry, agitated, scared, or in any other such state of heightened response, our breathing becomes rapid. It is a natural response of the body to get more oxygen so that our muscles can have more power for a proportionate response.

However, as we breathe, our breathing becomes short and rapid. We are inhaling and exhaling rapidly. It helps in supplying fresh oxygen fast and taking out the used air. The process is fueling us.

Deep breathing is the opposite process. It helps your body calm down. It distracts the mind from the issue and engages it with a crucial life process.

The Initiation

It is always better if you can sit down at someplace as that would help you calm down
You can do it while standing too
If you are standing, please take some support for better relaxation

Breathe out slowly and deeply
Allow as much air to come out of your body as possible
Be very slow and steady
Now, when you have exhaled completely
Begin inhaling slowly but deeply

We will do it once again

Breathe out slowly and deeply
Allow as much air to come out of your body as possible
Be very slow and steady
Now, when you have exhaled completely
Begin inhaling slowly but deeply

Now, bring your attention to your position
If you are sitting, please keep your back straight
You can use a backrest but do not use a neck rest
Keep your hands in your lap with palms facing upwards
You can also lie down if you feel like
Just keep your back straight at all times
You can also use a think but soft pillow
If you are standing, please keep your back straight
Do not slouch

If possible, close your eyes
If closing your eyes is not possible or you are feeling anxious
You can fix your eyes at any place in front of you
It can be any object

Breathe in
Breathe out

Breathe in
Breathe out

Breathe in
Breathe out

Do not try to control your breathing
Allow your breathing to attain a natural pace
You are in an agitated mental state
It is just a phase
It will pass
You are working towards it
Keep breathing naturally

Breathe in
Breathe out

Breathe in
Breathe out

Breathe in
Breathe out

There is no need to bother about anything
You are in a controlled state
You are addressing the situation
You are conscious of it
You are aware

Breathe in
Breathe out

Breathe in
Breathe out

Breathe in
Breathe out

Observe if your breathing is natural
If you are still breathing fast?
Relax!

Breathe in
Breathe out

Breathe in
Breathe out

We will do deep breathing now
It will help you calm down
Whatever you are feeling will pass
You will feel calm and composed
Your anger will dissipate
You will feel no angst
You can manage this

Breathe in
Breathe out

Breathe in
Breathe out

Now, breathe in from your nostrils
Very slowly
Please try to feel the air you are breathing in
Its temperature
Does it feel moist
The sensation it creates in your nostrils
We never care for this sensation
But, it can be felt
Keep breathing in slowly till you can
Do not force yourself

Hold your breath when you are full till your neck
Do not release it just yet
Please keep it tight
You might feel the pressure
It is bearable

Now, breathe out from your mouth
Very slowly
Even slowly than you breathed in
One step at a time
Push out all the air in your guts
Slowly but strongly exhale all the air

Relax!

Deep breathing is a very calming exercise
Please do not rush any part
Please keep your awareness tied to your breathing

Through your nostrils
Take a deep breath in
Very slowly and steadily
Feel the air
Through your awareness, follow it
Feel it filling up your body

Hold that air for a while
Allow the pressure to build
Let your awareness scan your body
Let it decimate every insecurity

Breathe out through your mouth
Very slowly
1..
2….
3…..
4…….

5.........
6..........
7.............
Excellent!

Feel the calm enveloping your mind
It swipes the mind
It feels great

You may still have thoughts
You don't need to worry about them
They are just thoughts
You are not your thoughts
You can stand aside and watch those thoughts
They have no control over you
You will allow them to pass
You will not engage
You will not get carried away
It is a phase
It will pass away

Again breathe in slowly from your nose
We will again do smaller inhalations and longer exhalations
Start inhaling from your nose to the count of 4
1
2
3
4
Hold your breath to the count of 4

1
2
3
4
Release the breath slowly through your mouth to the count of 7
1
2
3
4
5
6
7
Relax!

Now visualize your mind
Are you still feeling worried, anxious, stressed, or angry
Are these emotions still stirring you up
Do you have control over your mind
Relax!

Breathe in
Breathe out

Breathe in
Breathe out

Breathe in
Breathe out

Now bring your awareness back to your body
Feel your body
Try to feel the sensation of air touching your body
Become aware of the sounds in the background
Feel the fragrances in the air
Become fully aware of your sensations
Please do not open your eyes yet

Breathe in
Breathe out

Breathe in
Breathe out

We'll count backward to ten very slowly
You'll inhale and exhale slowly at every count
Be slow and steady do not rush
10
9
8
7
6
5
4
3
2
1
0
You can now become fully aware of the outside world

Thank You!

You can keep this breathing exercise as short as you want, or you can also make it as long as you wish. If you are in a personal space, deep breathing for longer is always more helpful. It gives you better control over your emotions. If you are feeling scared, agitated, or anxious, this exercise is very helpful.

Meditation

The Way to Untangle Your Thoughts

Meditation is the most effective tool for keeping the mind calm and decluttering your thoughts. People have a lot of misconceptions about meditation. It is not a standalone process that can help you in your life. It is only a way to understand your mind better. However, if you want greater transformation, you'll need to do much more than just meditation. The overall transformation requires lifestyle modifications so that meditation can be more effective.

Meditation is a very potent process. It can unravel the knots in our minds. We all have things in the past that may be unpleasant. But as we have already discussed, the mind never forgets everything. It saves the scariest of memories separately and plays them on a loop for us always to remember them. These are some of our biggest fears and insecurities. These are the traumatic events in the past that we don't want to deal with.

The mind knows that we are scared of dealing with them. It also knows that we may not be able to overcome such events or incidents in real-life, and hence it keeps playing them on a loop for us to remain mentally prepared. It is a defense mechanism. If you don't know how to swim, you may develop irrational fears of water. These fears help you stay away from water bodies, and you don't drown.

Such fears and anxieties help keep us safe from physical dangers, but when it comes to the recollection of traumatic events in the past, things get a little tricky. The mind is following a pattern. It isn't selective. The things it does for physical fears, it does the same with mental fears.

The things that make you fearful are your insecurities. They are the thoughts that you don't want to deal with. Those are the things you are ashamed of embarrassed of. However, there is no way you can work around them. If you want to lead a calm and peaceful life, you will have to address those feelings and emotions. You will have to meet your scarier thoughts midway and discard them.

Meditation is the medium that helps you accomplish that. The mind can exaggerate things as it wants you to be careful. Mental clutter can add layers to it and make you even more fearful. Decluttering the mind helps you in understanding those thoughts and addressing them. Once you have addressed those thoughts, they become powerless. They will not be able to affect your mental or emotional calm.

Objective Focus- The Sharpest Knife

One of the biggest disadvantages of having fearful thoughts is that they are always subjective. Your mind is never general; it is very specific. It always looks for your deepest and darkest insecurities. It has references. It knows when to play them. It is why you begin to get all the related negative thoughts whenever you are in a weak spot.

References help the mind in overcoming reason. It doesn't give a chance to your rationale to come into the argument.

Some thoughts have an ambush. They encircle you all of a sudden while others are on a siege. They are always surrounding you. But an important thing that never comes to the mind is that they are just thoughts. They aren't real. They are not based in reality. They are subjective.

Your mind can make you believe that your thoughts and you are the same. It is a very important thing that you must understand with great clarity.

Let us understand it with a different analogy.

When you were born, you were just a bundle of mass weighing only a few pounds. Today, you will be anywhere between 100 to 200 lbs. How did this magic happen?

The simple answer is that you ate, got nutrition, and you grew. That means a big part of you is that food. The banana, fish, cheese, and burgers that you might have consumed may have become you.

Does that mean you are that food?

No, you aren't that food. You processed it and changed it into a mass. Whatever couldn't become the mass was excreted. It was excrement.

Your thoughts are also the same. The unprocessed thoughts are like that food that has never been able to get processed. It is trying to become one. Your mind always tries to make you believe that you and your thoughts are the same. But both are separate.

We are our consciousness. The awareness you have is the real you. Everything else is an addition. Your intellect is also merely a tool. However, mental clutter can muddle this clarity. It can make you believe that you and your thoughts are the same.

Your subconscious mind, which has the most definitive collection of your thoughts and memories, becomes more powerful and overcomes your active mind. It even overshadows your intellect. It creates so much clutter that you are unable to discern facts from fiction.

Meditation is the way to overcome this hurdle.

Meditation doesn't mean simply sitting in a cross-legged posture and chanting something. It is a way to make your awareness look deep within the reaches of your conscious and subconscious mind to separate facts from fiction.

It is a way to address your thoughts and reason with them. Meditation is not an avoidance strategy. It is a definitive way to deal with your mental troubles.

When you meditate, you are not unconscious or subconscious; on the contrary, you are more aware than ever. You enable your awareness to look deep within and find the things that have been causing you distress.

Your awareness has an objective focus. It doesn't get swayed by emotions. It has the power to discern. It enables you to find the answers you have been looking for.

Meditation not only affects your thoughts, but it also influences your brain on a physical level.

The thoughts in your mind are chemical reactions and electrical synapses. The positive thoughts in your mind help in calming you down. They lead to the secretion of chemicals that can subdue negative emotions like anger and anxiety. When the production of negative thoughts reaches its threshold, the mind begins to produce stress hormones that can trigger a stress response, which is reactionary.

The nominal production of stress hormones is nothing bad. Your body can tolerate it. However, when you develop negative thought patterns, most of your thoughts are negative. It can lead to the continuous production of stress hormones, which is a chronic state.

Chronic stress can be more dangerous to you that you can think. It not only affects you mentally but physically.

Have you seen some people who are always worried about their weight but are unable to lose it? Such people can be suffering from chronic stress.

Chronic stress would lead to the secretion of cortisol hormone at a steady rate. This hormone can impair a lot of functions in the body. It can cause insulin resistance and several other hormonal changes. It will stall your weight loss and cause chronic lifestyle disorders like diabetes, high blood pressure, and cardiovascular disorders.

Meditation plays a big role in managing stress levels, and hence you can get relief from chronic stress. It eases your mind and the nervous system. Some regions in the brain are very helpful in decreasing anxiety and depression. Meditation can also help in increasing activity in these regions.

Meditation Can Help Physical Transformation of the Brain

In its agitated state, the mind produces beta waves. These are short-length electrical waves that are very fast and erratic. They lead to jumbled up thoughts, and you are continuously having a barrage of thought one after another. However, the meditative state is calming and produces slow alpha waves, which have a calming effect. They are not erratic or choppy, and hence you can find order in mind. It is important to note that alpha waves grow. Your mind learns to produce these waves as you practice. Initially, the alpha waves may be short, but the alpha waves keep getting longer and slower as you practice meditation. Finding peace and calm within yourself becomes easier.

Meditation has a positive impact on your mind psychologically and brings physiological changes in the brain.

Insular Cortex: This part of the brain is tasked with the awareness of breathing and heartbeat. Research has shown a positive increase in the insular cortex of long-term meditation practitioners. It means that if you practice meditation regularly, your awareness will deepen, and your heartbeat also becomes more stable. Your body can carry more oxygen and blood. It also enhances your immunity.

Premotor Cortex: This area regulates your emotions, thoughts, and attention span. Your ability to learn new things and your memory power is also regulated by it. The denser the grey matter in this region, the better will be your associated cognitive abilities. You will also have better control over your thoughts and emotions. Studies have found that meditation has a positive impact on this region and increases grey matter density.

Amygdala: This small almond-shaped cluster of cells may be small, but it is the center of all your fears, insecurities, stress, and anxieties. The denser the grey matter in your amygdala, the stress, anxiety, and fears will get triggered more frequently. Studies have positively concluded that meditation can help in lowering the grey matter in this region. It can help you become emotionally more stable.

Meditation is a powerful way to nourish your mind and enhance its abilities to fight the negativity. It doesn't cost you anything and doesn't require any specific preparation. You can do it all alone in the calm and peace of your mind, or you can also do it in a group. No matter how you do it, the effect will always be positive.

Some people like to meditate in the morning while others like to do that in the evening. It is your mind, and you are free to treat it anytime you want.

The only thing that you must never forget is that meditation is also a tool to help you declutter your mind. It helps you have an objective look at your thoughts and lowers your levels of anxiety and fear.

You can become more aware and focused. You'll know the problems to address. However, you'll still need to make several lifestyle changes and clear the clutter physically and mentally. You will also need to develop a mindful and minimalist approach to detect negative thought patterns and alter them consciously.

Meditation is not a complete solution. It is only a part of the solution. Most people begin meditation as a medium to declutter their minds and then get disappointed when they don't find a long-term solution.

It happens because they are trying to stitch using a sword.

Our intellect is a sword. It has the power to discern. It can separate black from white. If you have thoughts, it can understand their meanings. But, if you only have thoughts but take no action, the scope of this sword will be limited.

If you meditate but do not alter your procrastination habit, the clutter would keep increasing as it is. The more you sort, the more you'll get. It will become a sore job.

If you have clutter all around you, you will feel the same amount of suffocation. Your mind will always remain overstimulated and have poor focus.

If your relationships are cluttered, you will find it hard to do anything as there will be a constant tussle in your mind. There will be no space for calm. You'll only keep struggling with your thoughts, and even meditation would also provide temporary relief from those thoughts. It would make even meditation a part of your avoidance strategy.

If you do not declutter your online presence, you will keep absorbing the same amount of clutter all the time. Your thoughts and emotions would keep getting triggered by several unrelated things, and maintaining focus would become even more difficult.

Therefore, you must use meditation as a part of your metal declutter strategy but never use it as a standalone weapon and expect outstanding results.

Reasons to Practice Meditation

It Brings Happiness: Inner peace and happiness have become a rare commodity in this age. Do you remember the time as a child when you didn't need anything to be happy? As a child, we used to be happy on our own. We could play with the same toys again and again. We could get cheerful looking at our parents without any expectations. Don't you think all that has changed now? We need assistance to be happy. We need people to tell us jokes so that we can feel cheerful. It has happened because we have lost connection with the areas in our brain that make us exuberant. The clutter in our mind overshadows those areas. When you meditate, you can uncover them and feel happy again. You would need no reason to make you happy. For us, human beings, unhappiness should need a reason, and we have made it the exact opposite. Meditation helps you reverse that process. It instills a calm inside you.

It Will Reduce Anxiety, Anger, Stress, and Hopelessness: As we have already discussed above, there are several areas in the brain triggered by meditation that can help in lowering stress, anxiety, anger, and hopelessness. The more you meditate, the better will be your control over these emotions.

Relief From the Word Get-Go: Every procedure takes some time to show results. However, meditation is an instant relief pill that begins showing its impact from the first day. If you feel highly agitated, stirred, or anxious, try meditation for a while, and you'll understand how powerful the process is.

Better Sleep Regulation: Sleep difficulties are not uncommon for people with a cluttered mind. They are never able to unfold their thoughts. Meditation can help them address the things that are plaguing the mind at the moment. We have a poor distinction between ruminating and thinking. Most of the time, we are just thinking in circles without an attempt to conclude. It is overthinking. Meditation can help you break free from this pattern.

Sharper Memory: Our mind is a large storehouse of thoughts without a proper inventory system. The indexing mechanism of thoughts is poor. It can lead to poor memory. Meditation helps you remember things better because you can use your consciousness to index important things properly.

Clarity and Focus: Lack of clarity and focus are also major problems for people with a cluttered mind. They are never able to build a perspective. Meditation helps them see clearly, and gain a better perspective.

Meditation is all about practice. You'll keep getting better at it as you practice more. We will now practice a meditation session that would focus on understanding the thoughts and bring self-awareness.

Guided Meditation

Preparation

Please take a seat
Become comfortable
Let your body and mind relax completely
Initially, anything and everything may become a distraction
You do not need to bother
Those are temporary distractions
It is preferable to wear loose-fitting, comfortable clothes

Initially, when you sit for meditation
Your mind may wander here and there
Several thoughts may come swarming
No matter how hard you try to resist
It'll still happen

Please do not pay attention to it
However, it is always a good idea to sit with a pen and paper
In the initial few minutes while you are relaxing
If anything important crosses your mind
Write that down on paper
Do not try to store it in your mind as it'll keep coming back
Such thoughts cause the greatest distraction

Use a comfortable cushion for sitting
Uncomfortable seating position can keep drawing your attention
For meditation, the full lotus position is usually the best
However, it can be difficult for many people
Try to sit normally in a cross-legged position

During the meditation session
You'll need to keep your back upright
If you slouch, you may feel lazy or distracted
If you want, you can use a backrest

Please keep your neck straight
But, never use a neck rest
Also, keep your chin raised a little

Please sit straight but do not make your body stiff
Keep your shoulders parallel to each other
You can keep your hand on your knees or even in your lap

Keep your palms facing upwards
Ensure that there is no physical stress
Make adjustments of position by leaning forward and sideways a few times

(Now give yourself a few minutes to relax. Do not rush this time. Use this time to calm the mind or to allow your thoughts to settle. If you have anything specific in your mind, write it down.)

Initiation

Please ensure that you are comfortable and relax
Now, close your eyes gently
There is no reason to think anything
Close your eyes and relax

Do not feel stressed
You do not need to do anything
You do not need any preparation
You only need to relax

Do not bother about the procedure
Do not bother about the duration
Relax completely
You do not even need to control your mind
Do not try to shun the thoughts
They'll become ferocious
If your mind is running in all directions
Stop paying attention

Your awareness and your thoughts are not the same
Your thoughts can do their thing
It won't matter
You only need your awareness to keep you calm
If you are having thoughts
Acknowledge those thoughts
But do not engage with them
Do not try to ponder about them
But, do not even try to overlook them
Accept that you are having thoughts
Then shift your awareness to the task at hand
It is a simple process
You'll see this just in a bit

Bring your awareness to your breathing
Do not try to control your breath
You do not need to hold your breath
There is no need to breathe deeply, just yet
Keep breathing as you are
Observe your breathing carefully
If you are breathing fast
Calm down
Keep your awareness on your breath
It will relax in a few minutes
At this point, we are not trying to control anything
You only need to observe
It would help if you looked at everything with close attention
You need to pay attention to detail
Feel the things you might not have felt important

Everything is important
All the senses are important
Now we will bring awareness to all the senses

Thoughts may come rushing to your mind
There is nothing to worry
You do not need to pay attention to them
It is not the time to address them

You need to feel your body now
Bring your awareness to your body
With your eyes closed, try to feel your limbs
Through your awareness, feel your belly
Scan your complete spine with your awareness

It is time to hear the sounds in your background
Pay very close attention to any sound you can hear
From the ticking of the clock to the whirring of the air-conditioning
Try to pick the faintest noise you can get
When your mind is calm, the ability to hear increases manifolds
Can you hear anything specific?

Now, bring your focus to the smells around you
Can you feel any fragrance?
Do it without judgment
Don't think about good or bad fragrance
Do not bother even about its likeability
Only try to smell anything you can

Try to feel your body as a whole
Sense anything you are feeling on your body
Can you feel the clothes touching your body?
Do you feel any tingling?

Now focus your awareness inwards
Try to scan your whole body through it
Do you feel any stress, tension, or fatigue
Are you feeling tired, tensed, or stiff
Do you feel any pressure

Awareness is a great medium
It has no limitations
It enables you to look inwards and outwards
Nothing is hidden from your awareness
All you need is intent

Scan your whole body
From tip to toe
Try to feel the areas of pressure and pain
You do not need to do anything, but acknowledge and accept
Do not try to ignore it
(Take a few minutes to scan your body)

Meditation

Bring your awareness to your breathing
There is no need to control it
Just observe

Watch the breath coming in
Then observe it going out

It is such a crucial process
We can't live without it
Yet, we seldom pay attention to it

A breath in
A breath out

A breath in
A breath out

A breath in
A breath out

It is such a simple process
You do not need to learn it
You know it before you are born

As long as you live
The process of breathing in and breathing out continues
One day it stops
And, we bid our goodbye to this mortal world
Yet, all our lives we are never thankful for the process of breathing
We worry so much about our weight all our lives
We worry so much about the way we look
But, never about the way we breathe
You miss a few breaths, and the story is over
You can extend your life by paying attention to the breath

Yet, it remains out of focus
Mental clutter does that to us

Keep your focus on your breathing
Pay attention to every breath you are taking
Let it be rhythmic
Pay attention to the rhythm of your heart
With a calm mind, you can hear your heartbeat
The music is magical

As your breathing becomes calm
It gets it rhythm
Your body would begin to relax completely
You'll have better focus

Now, we will practice deep breathing
It is an exercise to focus your awareness completely
You'll have the control
You will be able to feel it

We will take a slow but deep breath through the nostrils
You'll inhale to the count of 4

Then, hold that breath to the count of 5
Allow the fresh air to assimilate in your blood

Finally, we will release the breath from the mouth
We'll do it even slowly
Keep breathing out till the count of 7

Your awareness should remain with your breath

You may have thoughts
You may get distracted
Acknowledge the thoughts
But, bring your awareness back to your breathing

You can repeat this process as many times as you need
It will help you calm down completely
It will allow you to achieve complete focus

Breath in through your nostrils
1..
Begin breathing in slowly
2….
Please do not rush the process
3…..
Observe the air entering your nostrils
4………
Please try to observe the way it feels

Now,
Hold your breath
1..
You'll feel an unusual calm within you
2….
The calm has always been there
3……
The clutter prevents us from feeling it
4………
Observe the way you feel now
5…………

Look deep within you

Finally,
It is time to exhale slowly through your mouth
1..
Very slowly, start releasing your breath
2…..
Do not rush the process
3……
You might have the urge to release the pressure
4………
Exhale slowly; it will help you drive out your worries
5………..
Even when you feel you have exhaled, push some more
6……………
Exhale to make way for fresh air
7………………
Push till your belly deflates completely

Relax!

The calm after deep breathing is different
It is the calm of control
You regain complete control of your awareness
Your mind stops wandering
It becomes focused

We will practice deep breathing once again
Inhale slowly and steadily

1.. Feel the air you are breathing in and the way it stimulates your nostrils
2.... Imagine the air entering your body with a light
3..... Follow this light and observe the way the air fills your body
4....... Feel the way it inflates your chest, lungs, and the stomach

Hold your breath now
1.. There will be calm
2.... You'll also feel the pressure building inside you
3..... This pressure is good
4....... Your body will struggle to push the spent air out
5.......... Bear the pressure, only a bit more

Now, exhale through your mouth very slowly
1.. Very slowly, allow the air to pass out through your mouth
2.... Do not rush
3......Take your time in pushing out the spent air
4........Observe your stomach deflate
5.......... Push it even harder
6............ Feel your belly going deep towards your back
7............... Exhale all the air to make way for fresh air

Relax!

Observe your mind now
You will find no thoughts
There will be nothing distracting your mind

How to Declutter Your Mind

Nothing to make you worried

Breathe in
Breathe out

Breathe in
Breathe out

Breathe in
Breathe out

Your awareness is in control
You are calm and composed
Bring your awareness to your thoughts
Your thoughts and your awareness are not the same
Both are different entities
Through your awareness, look at your thoughts
The way they form
Do not judge your thoughts
Only observe the way they form in your mind
It is a continuous process
It happens on your own
Do not engage with your thoughts
Please do not attach labels to them
There is no need to curse yourself for having those thoughts
It is an automated process

Till the time you remain indifferent to the thoughts
They will not affect you
You can discard them

You can move ahead
You can have negative thoughts
You can have positive thoughts
You are not those thoughts
They are just a creation of the mind
You have the control of the mind
You can shut these thoughts
You can even change them
You can shift your awareness any moment you want

Let us broaden the scale of your awareness
Let us focus your awareness on physical discomfort
Through your awareness, scan the things that cause physical discomfort
Does this thought make you wince?
Did you notice that there was no real pain?
You just felt it through your awareness

Did you notice that the pain was not imaginary?
You are fully awake
You are not in sleep
You can feel the pain while it is not there
It is the trick your mind plays with you
It recollects pain and unpleasant experiences fast
It makes you feel these as if they are real
Such things influence your real-life decisions

You can avoid that
You can overcome this thinking
You can break this make-believe world

You can even take your mind off these thoughts

Your mind is imagining thoughts
It creates them
It gives them references
They are a reflection of past events
Still, they are just reflections
Creation of your mind
But, your awareness is objective
It can discern
It can differentiate and distinguish
Real from unreal
It can evaluate

You do not need to fear your thoughts
Let us once again get back to your thoughts
Observe your thoughts
Label them as good or bad
Don't think of good or bad thoughts
Label the ones you are having at the moment
Do not judge yourself for having those thoughts
(Long Pause)

Do you still feel bad about these thoughts?
Do you still fear them?
Do you think they can harm you?

Thoughts are thoughts
They do not have the power
We make them powerful by believing in them

We delegate power to them
You can take that power back, anytime

You don't have to fight thoughts
There is no need to contemplate
Just label them as good or bad and move on
Keep your awareness on the reality
Become objective
Do not let your thoughts drive you on fear
Do not let them have more power over you

Think of people you know
Think of the things you don't like in them
Think of the things you like in them
Can you like them more?
Can you be more compassionate?
Can you become more tolerant?
Think of the things that agitate you
Can you help yourself better?
Can you control your mood?
Everything is inside you
You can control everything related to you
You only need to become aware

Now become aware of the things you feel when speaking to others
Think of your fears
Think of your worries
Think of the insult you might face
Think of the way others would mock

Now become aware that all that isn't real
You are making up all that in your mind
It was never real
There is no basis for this fear
No base for these thoughts
Become aware of the feelings

You are aware now
You know that you are in control
Your thoughts can't dictate you
Your mind can't run you
You are in complete command

Now bring your awareness to your thoughts
You don't have to participate
You are here to observe
Just look at the thoughts
They are not you
They don't reflect what you are
The thoughts in your mind are not a reflection of you

Simply observe your thought
Identify a thought that strikes you the most
Focus on it
Watch that thought closely
Do you identify it
Do you feel any emotion with this thought

Watch the form that thought takes
You don't need to change it

There needs to be no indulgence
Your participation is not required
Simply look at it

The mind has so many thoughts
They are not even connected
There is no reason to be concerned

Just maintain non-judgmental Observation
There is no reason to judge your thoughts
You don't need to bother about the kind of thoughts you have
No one is judging you
You also don't need to judge
You can pick and drop these thoughts
They are just like objects
There is no need for attachment
There is no need for resentment
Observe them
The form they take
How they come and go
Watch the speed of formation of thoughts
Observe the way they disappear
They aren't permanent
There is no reason to fear them
They are the creation of your mind
They have no physical form
You can make them disappear
Feel the power within you

Bring awareness back to your breathing
Watch the rhythm of your breathing
Is it stable
Are you breathing fast
Let it gain a natural pace

Now with your eyes closed
Focus your awareness outside
Try to feel your body
Feel the air on your skin
Does it feel warm or cold?
Try to move your toes
Do you feel it?
There can be a tingling sensation
Don't bother
It will go away

Breathe in
Breathe out

Breathe in
Breathe out

You are feeling calm now
You have a truce with your thoughts
They are not your enemies
But your thoughts do not rule you
Feel the calm in your heart
You are relaxed now
You can open your eyes when ready

Thank You!

Mindfulness

Mindfulness, as you know, is the quality of living in the present. Physically, it isn't possible to live at any other time than the present, but mentally and emotionally, most of us live in the past and the future.

Past events and incidents highly influence our actions, thoughts, and beliefs. Most people spend all their lives regretting what they couldn't do in the past while others regret the things they did. People can have their reasons, but the past has a huge influence on our lives.

The more we focus on our past, the most worried we are about our future. While the past may invoke fear, the future invokes anxiety. We miss out on the present when we begin thinking about the future. Most of the time, we base our future on our past and do not give any significance to the present action.

That's why living in the present can be a big deal.

Do you relate to the following:

- Past events influence your present decisions
- When you are making a decision, you are unable to think of the past
- Your experiences in the past lead to prejudices
- There are things in the past that can make you shudder even today
- You are carrying some baggage of the past on your mind

These are not random things. They are real. No matter who you are, the past influences us. It must influence us as it gives us a chance to learn.

It is why we all study history. It gives us a chance to know the mistakes that our elders created and the things they led to. However, history is a study of cause and effect. It is not a thing to memorize days and names. You need to understand that when two people fight for dominance, there can be bloodshed, that fact that so and so fought and lost blood is of no significance.

In the same way, you made a decision, and it leads to poor results. It should be a lesson. That action must not become a permanent fixture in your memory. Unfortunately, this is what happens eventually. We store every action with reference, and then our mind keeps revisiting those events again and again.

It is a trap that can only become even more painful. We become such a slave of our memories and thoughts that we begin to live there. We stop taking any action. We keep ruminating over the possible outcomes of any action to discard it for a lack of approval ultimately.

Living in the Mind

'Living in mind' is an actual phenomenon. If you look around and even within you, it wouldn't be very difficult to find a score of people living in their minds. They are always making plans, supposing things, and then not able to must the courage to execute them.

People post pictures and memories on social media platforms and, within minutes, begin to calculate their foes and friends based on social media posts. They do not allow some time to pass. They do not try to know the reason for delays in response. They have their mind ready with its arsenal of assumptions and thoughts.

These are also very important reasons for mental clutter. We are giving constant fodder to our minds to assume things, and we rely on those assumptions to make them more believable.

It is somewhat like the media trials conducted by the news channels. If you think that the media channels also thought that way, you are wrong. They are smart people.

Clever enough to know the direction of the wind. They guess the public sentiment and run stories that favor those thoughts. The popular sentiment was already leaning on that side, and when they see news media channels also saying the same, they develop confirmation bias.

They still believe what they had assumed in the evening; they are just leaning on the news channels for support. There is no logic. There is no deduction.

In our current state of the cluttered mind, we are also moving in the same way. We have biases. We have prejudices. We have contempt. We have resentment. We have regrets, and we display all that in our thoughts, calling them organic.

If you want to declutter your mind, You will have to learn to Live in the present.

Living in the Present

Mindfulness is the process of living in the present. It is a very simple way of life in which you stop living by your memories and begin to experience, sense, observe, and reason things.

It is a process of living with your awareness. You stop leading your life on autopilot. There can be no denying that we are judgmental, lazy, and distracted in our decisions.

The Malady of Being Judgmental

Our dependence on past experiences is so high that we fail to have new experiences in our lives. We cannot know some people better or more about their good qualities because we base our opinion on a single bad incident with that person. Such incidents can have various reasons, but our minds cannot break past events' memories. It is the disease of being judgmental from which most of us suffer to a great extent. It can cripple our thought process to a great extent. It can begin extrapolating incidents that may never materialize. But their fears will always remain real.

Judgmental attitude is a great impediment in the way of living in the present. It makes you base all your conclusion on past events and experiences and do not consider the present's unique circumstances.

Living mindfully or living in the present includes a logical analysis of the present conditions and forming your decision based on them. It removes all biases and makes you act as per the current situation.

Life without judgment opens us doors to new experiences and relationships. You are not fearful of things based on your prior experiences, and you are prepared to give it a fresh try based on current facts of the matter. It is a better way to make decisions as your decisions aren't based on decade-old experiences when the situations might have been different.

Freedom from Laziness

Ruminating thing is an excuse to take time to sit ideally and think. When you are not living mindfully, you are wasting too much time thinking about things. You want to scan your memory and base your decisions on them. You want to inspect and over inspect things, and that leads to even more laziness. It leads to a loss of precious time.

When you are living mindfully, all the facts are always in front of you, and there is nothing that you need to gather to make your decisions. You have fewer excuses to procrastinate, and life becomes fast and easy. The clutter in your routine decreases, and your mind is free to think about new things.

Distractions

Our thoughts can be very distracting. They have a knack of jumping from one point to another. It doesn't allow us to focus on one point completely. Their awareness is weak, and they are not able to differentiate between facts and their fears.

This kind of living can lead to several difficulties and clutter for sure. The more you live in mind, the more you'll rely on mental clutter.

Mindfulness is the way of living in which you base your actions on facts and choose to live consciously.

Living Consciously

For most people, conscious living can be a difficult choice in the beginning. We are habitual of living on autopilot. Most of our actions are out of habit.

- Have you ever paid attention to the way you eat?
- Have you ever paid attention to the way you think?
- Have you ever paid attention to the way you walk?
- Have you even paid attention to the way you talk?

I can pose hundreds of such questions, and the answer to all those questions would be a 'no.'

It is not your fault.

Our race has been moving ahead at such a pace that it wants to jump ladders. The crème de la crème of the society has perfected the art of paying attention. It is focused. It is secure and confident.

The people below them are just ambitious. They aspire to reach there but follow the wrong path. They think that they can reach there by multitasking or doing too many things.

They forget the amount of distance the successful people have traveled and the time they have taken. Even an average Joe wants to make up for all that time and distance by multitasking and presents it as the key to success.

When you are multitasking, your focus is not even on one thing. You are just thinking that you are doing too many things while you are not accomplishing anything.

Mindful living means paying attention to every aspect of life. When you eat, you feel the food, savor it, and get its nutrition. When you talk, you pay attention to every word said by the other person and respond with only what is required and apt. Mindful walking means walking with consciously. It is much more than dragging your weight on this earth.

In summary, mindfulness is living consciously.

You do not allow your thoughts or habits to take over your awareness. You do not ruminate over things but make decisions based on facts.

Path to Become Mindful

Mindfulness can seem to be a very difficult way of life to adapt as you need to remain aware of all your actions all the time. However, it isn't easy to adapt until you are thinking of finding a quick fix. It is a way of life. The moment you accept it as a way of life and begin practicing it, you'd find that it is not only easy but very organized.

Mindfulness can help you eliminate most of the mental clutter in your life, and it will also bring you out of the autopilot mode. You will have complete control over the direction of your life as well as your decision. Your decisions will no more get swayed by memories or events. You will not remain a victim of your memories.

If you want to adapt Mindfulness, there are four main principles that you must follow:

Deep Breathing

We have covered deep breathing in some detail. It is a very helpful and effective way to remain in the present and get over the surge of emotions that may overwhelm your senses.

You can practice deep breathing as a standalone procedure. However, if you want to make it a way of life and improve your control of breath and senses, you can also practice Yoga. Yoga has several deep breathing exercises like Pranayama that can help you a lot.

Practicing deep breathing can help you in achieving the following four objectives:

1. Improved stress response of the body due to focused breathing
2. Control over frequent anger flare-ups
3. Better control over PTSD and other stress and anxiety-related disorders
4. Improvement in physical health and endurance

Most people fear that practicing deep breathing means that they'll need to keep pumping breath out like chronic asthma patients all the time. It is a process of awareness. You only need to remain aware of your breath whenever you can. You neither need to control your breath nor change anything in the beginning. All you are required to do is maintain awareness about your breath.

Our breathing is a very conscious process. If your focus is on breathing, your mind will remain focused, and your breathing would remain rhythmic and deep.

Physical Awareness

Physical awareness or awareness of your body is a crucial part of mindfulness.

Our conscious effort is to live in the present. While your mind is always bumping chaotically between the past and the future, your body can only live in the present. There is no way for the body to move at any other time. If you keep your awareness tied to your body, it will become much easier for you to live in the present.

As you know, almost 95 percent of all our actions are automated. We do them by force of habit. Things happen like an impulse action. You don't have to use your mind or discretionary power to do those actions.

If you want to develop physical awareness or awareness of your body, you will have to change that. Meditation and deep breathing are very helpful processes that can help you in it.

There are some simple exercises for developing physical awareness. Regularly practicing them will make it easier for you to become more aware or conscious of your body and the need to remain in the present.

Deep breathing and a non-judgmental attitude are crucial parts of the following exercise:

Physical Awareness Exercise

Sit with your back straight
Sitting in a cross-legged posture is better
You can also sit on a chair
Please ensure that the palms of your feet are firmly on the ground
Keep your knees straight
Close your eyes and focus on your breathing
Observe your breathing carefully
Do not try to alter it yet
Only observe the pace of your breathing

Inhale
Exhale

When you close your eyes, several thoughts may arise
Your awareness may flicker
Do not resist your thoughts
Acknowledge them
But bring your awareness back to your breathing
Allow your breathing to become rhythmic

Visualize the air entering your body
Traveling throughout the body
Energizing it
And then
Exiting through your mouth

Inhale
Exhale

Now shift your awareness to your thoughts
Focus on the thoughts at present
Acknowledge them
Do not judge them
They can be positive
They can be negative
They can be about you
They can be about others
Thoughts are flimsy
They are not real
They are a creation of your mind
Your mind can think whatever it wants
But you are not your thoughts
You are not even this body
You are just this awareness
You are this consciousness

Focus your awareness to the center of your thoughts
Look at numerous thoughts there
They are in various stages of development
A thought takes birth and vanishes

All happens in this mind
They have no physical form
Your mind accepts them and makes them strong
You have the power to push them away
They are not powerful

Observe them
But no not engage
You are a mere spectator
Watch them form and disappear
Do not judge these thoughts
Judgment will lead to engagement

Now shift your awareness to your emotions
Are you feeling happy?
Are you feeling sad?
Are you feeling sorry
Do not judge these states
Only observe the emotional state
Become aware of your emotions
Do not discard them
Acknowledge them
But do not engage

Now bring your awareness back to your breathing
Through your awareness, feel your body
Try to feel every sensation
The way your clothes are fluttering over your skin
The way the air in the room feels
The light that you can feel with your eyes closes

The temperature
The humidity in the air or the dryness
Just feel
Do not engage
Do not react
Only try to feel any sensation you might have
Through your awareness, scan your body from top to bottom
With your eyes closed, you can see whatever you like
Try to absorb any pain, stress, anxiety in any part
If you notice, acknowledge it
Accept that sensation
Allow your sensation to heal it

Bring your awareness back to your breathing
You are breathing slow and steady
You are calm
You are relaxed
Please open your eyes gently
Physical awareness exercise is easy and relaxing. It helps you relax your mind and your body. It also allows you to form a connection between your awareness and your physical body. You can practice it whenever you feel unsettled.

Awareness of Thoughts

The human mind is a thought machine. It can have thousands of thoughts a day. On average, you could be having a thought per second for the whole 86,400 seconds of the day.

We have an active or conscious mind that is responsible for making operational decisions. We also have a subconscious mind that processes information. However, both differ in their information processing abilities. The conscious mind processes information at 40-60 bits per second. The active mind recognizes and analyses information, and hence its processing abilities are slower.

Some researchers believe that the subconscious mind can process information at a rate of 40o million bits per second. There can be no comparison between the processing abilities of both the mind.

Here, it is also important to note that the active mind's participation in overall brain activity is a mere 0.1 percent. The subconscious mind does the remainder of the work. It is responsible for responding to the 50 trillion cells in the body and their impulses. The subconscious brain activity is similar to playing 10,000 movies at once. The data rate is a whopping 320GB/sec.

Therefore, it is natural that your subconscious mind's thought production abilities will always be higher than the conscious mind. Your subconscious mind is always at work. While your conscious mind is only active during your waking hours, the subconscious is working till you are alive. For it, there are no breaks, no relaxation, and no napping. That's the reason it is such a formidable adversary when it comes to mental clutter.

It maintains a very large pool of data and keeps playing it on a loop. The subconscious mind helps form habits, routines, reflexes, and all such things that would not require your brain's active participation.

In an age when humankind is running toward automation, this advice may look filled with prejudice against the mind running us on autopilot. However, there is more than meets the eye.

The role of the subconscious is only to instill habits, routines, and reflexes. It doesn't differentiate whether the habits are good or bad. If you have developed a positive thought pattern, the subconscious will reinforce even those. However, the problem is that when these habits are forming in your growing years, you may not have the kind of discretion to pick the right ones.

Breaking negative thought patterns and forming new habits are the tasks that you would need to rewrite on the subconscious. That's why you must have an awareness of your thoughts.

Our conscious mind makes critical decisions. It is not responsible for passive decisions like controlling the functioning of the organs. But the interaction of the mind with the thoughts is an activity that involves your conscious mind. It evokes reactions. It generates emotions. If you allow your passive mind to regulate that, your life can get out of control, and that's what has been happening.

The subconscious mind has a crucial role to play. It is the long-term memory that also helps you avoid dangers, falling into traps, or repeating similar mistakes. However, these constructive roles can take a backseat when you give complete control to the subconscious mind. It may start playing fearful memories in a loop to prevent any action so that you may never face danger, but that's not the correct way to live and progress.

All this can be avoided if you develop an awareness of thoughts. Awareness of thoughts is a key component of cultivating mindfulness.

All that you are required to do is remain aware of:

- Thoughts in your mind that are leading to another and then to another
- The thoughts that are evoking a severe emotional response from you
- The highly agitating thoughts making you feel dreadful or stunned
- It would help if you especially remained aware of impulsive thoughts

If you want your mind to remain sharp, focused, and effective, awareness of thought is important. It is the only way to prevent you from getting trapped in the virtual world of your subconscious thoughts.

Your mind has a massive memory bank that can keep playing your contextual memories and keep you engaged with the past. It has only one problem; you will remain thinking and not make decisions. It is a path that leads to inaction or passive action. You will remain in a reactionary mode, which is beyond your control.

We are living in the age of information overload. We are continuously getting bombarded by some information all the time. It has an impact on our thinking. The subconscious mind keeps getting clued and begins a new train a thought based on that information.

You might feel that you are just pondering over the information, but your mind relates to that information and references reality. It is an additional engagement that could have been avoided.

Information is only a trigger for the subconscious. The more useless information you grab, the higher will be the unwanted engagement.

The following things can help you in better thought awareness:

Practice Detachment: Detachment is a heavy word but an important word. We easily get identified with several things around us. Our job, our friends, our identity, our choices, our desires, our leaning, and many such things become a part of our identity. It leads to too much attachment, and we are constantly worried about one thing or another. Thought awareness is about not getting identified with these things. Your job is important, but it isn't you. If you get too mentally attached to it, any minor turbulence in your job will make your life off-balance. Mental detachment is very important. You must pay attention to everything you are doing but not carry it on your mind all the time.

You should not rely on material things like your smartphone, your TV time, or your car so much that you do not have the time to think beyond these.

Breath Awareness: Awareness of your breath is another way to create thought awareness of your thought. Whenever your mind begins an unending chain of thoughts, focusing on your breath can help.

Non-Judgmental Attitude: A big reason we remain in thoughts is that we are judgmental of most of the things and people around us. When we are judging something, it leads to mental engagement. Your mind begins to make references. You must avoid judging things. Accept the way they are and act accordingly.

Stop Multi-tasking: Do not multi-task. It has become a disease these days. People can't stick to one thing at one time. Multi-tasking cannot help you do things fast. It only causes distraction.

Let Go of Negative Thoughts and Emotions

We all have things in the past that may make us giggle, frown, sulk, and fear. It is natural to have so. Life is an eventful journey, and it is bound to have all kinds of experiences. However, when you keep living all those experiences again and again in your mind, you have little scope to live in the real world.

Most of us can only recall a good incident of the past that can make us giggle only once in a while. However, you may keep getting thoughts of fearful incidents in the past all the time.

It happens because your mind keeps playing them back so that you remain careful. Those things have happened. They are not going to happen now. You are so afraid of them that you are not addressing them. All of this will lead to mental clutter.

Letting such thoughts go is the only way you can find peace within you and get freedom from mental clutter.

The past has happened. In the present, if you are ruminating about it, that's mental clutter.

If you let go of these thoughts, you will become more mindful as there will be more space for attention and focus.

Breath awareness, physical awareness, thought awareness, and freedom from the cobweb of your memories are the four pillars that can help develop a mindfulness attitude.

Chapter 12: Decluttering Your Life and Responsibilities

Have you ever tried calling yourself from your mobile phone?

It always tells you are busy. In reality, you are doing nothing.

All of us are always busy but accomplishing nothing. We are getting nowhere. We have become Sysiphus, who is tasked with doing an unending task. We have no time for our family; we have no time for other people, and we don't even have time for ourselves.

This feigned engagement is also a clutter that needs to be cleared. It is one of the biggest impediments in your progress up the career path.

We have discussed the importance of breaking the chains of mental barriers. It is crucial for liberating you truly. Until you do that, nothing can make you feel truly free.

- Do you long for the weekend on the first day of the week?
- Are you constantly thinking about taking short breaks?
- Do you begin to look at the watch for lunch hour even when you aren't hungry?
- Are you always looking at the clock for the office to be over while you have nothing interesting planned even after that?
- Are you looking for an escape but don't know from what?

If the answer to some of these questions is affirmative, you are feeling bound within your mind. You have so many things keeping you tied in your mind that you will never feel free even if you are given a very long vacation.

Your problem is not with work or objectives but the way you have put them in suspended animation.

This attitude can lead to procrastination and confusion. It is also one of the biggest contributors to mental clutter besides emotions originating from thoughts.

We all have responsibilities in life, but some of us seem to have all too many. We always remain riddled with the worries of the pending work. We always feel that we are doing more but not getting enough in return or not getting the due credit. We feel stuck in a position, stature, or box, and there is no way out.

We look at others and see them liberated and enjoying, and it makes us feel even worse.

If you have these thoughts all the time, you urgently need to sort your life and responsibilities. Your work or your responsibilities in life that are not holding you back. You are the prisoner of your mind. It is becoming a trap, and you are feeling claustrophobic inside it.

It usually happens when your priorities are not set, and you are swinging between choices. In such a condition, you lose clarity of vision and begin to muddle things into one another.

Some of the ways you can deal with these are:

Prioritize What Really Matters

One of the biggest problems that we face in our lives is that we don't have clear priorities. We are leading lives idealized by others. Our parents, society, peers, our desires present something as a better option, and we set that as a priority in life. We work a big portion of our lives on it and then feel disillusioned because that was never our priority.

People with no empathy for others want to become a doctor. Their main objective is money. Money can bring comfort. But, would it also bring inner happiness and peace. What if that person enjoyed singing more.

It was just an example of career priorities. We make several such compromises in our daily lives. Some people pay more attention to their work and neglect family. The purpose was to earn more money to have joy in life. The strained personal and family life will ultimately ruin their personal life and drive out joy.

Some people are jugglers. They are never able to determine what is important for them in reality. They want to do everything and give time to all. They are in greater trouble as nothing gets the attention due.

Priorities can't be too many. Warren Buffet says that you can't have too many priorities in life as they do not remain priorities. They can be dreams, desires, aspirations, but not priorities.

As per Buffet, you should list all the most important objectives you have in life and then narrow it down to 5. Strikeout everything else. Do not even keep them for later. Eliminate them from your mind as this life is too short for doing too many things. When you have this level of clarity, you'll be able to deal with clutter better.

Lay Focus on Your Core Values to Avoid Deviation and Dilemma

Our core values matter to us the most. No matter how we may behave in the outside world, we can never ignore our core values. There a few things we truly believe in and others we follow or support because others expect that. When we lead such a life, clutter will come naturally.

There needs to be uniformity between your core values and what you do for decluttering life and your responsibilities. We may think that we are only pretending certain things in life, but our mind processes everything, and such contradictions lead to clutter.

When you deviate from your core values, you'll face dilemmas at every step, and decision fatigue will become an integral part of you.

The best way to avoid clutter in life and your responsibilities is always to follow your core principles.

Become More Objective and Bring Clarity of Vision

You might have seen some people working in a state of trance. They are not worried about anything or anyone, and their objective focus is on their way. Do you think those people are worried about minor issues around them like the fan making noise or someone having a tea beside them?

Some are only troubled even with trivial things around them. When they do something even more trivial, it is natural for the mind to look for an excuse to break free.

When you become objective in life, there is greater clarity. You can focus better.

Most of us lose this objectivity in life and our responsibility. We are always looking at things subjectively. We first attach our opinion and beliefs to those things and then begin our analysis. The whole process then becomes cloudy, and it is not going to yield good results.

If you want to bring clarity in your life and your responsibilities, you will have to objectively look at your main goals. You must focus on them and leave aside everything else.

Set Goals Mindfully

The mindful setting of goals is another important thing you need to consider. When you are setting your goals, you shouldn't get swayed by your emotions, desires, or assumptions.

Your goals need to have clarity as they are going to drive you ahead. An unrealistic goal will never evoke deep emotion inside you.

On the eve of the new year, millions of people make new year resolutions. On the next day of January, the resolution dies a silent and humiliating death for most people.

Why do these resolutions fail?

They are made in peer pressure. The whole world is making resolutions, and hence even you resolve. You want it to be better than others, and hence you set even tougher targets. It is always an exercise in futility.

If you want your life goals to work, they must always be within reach and planned meticulously. Mindful setting up of goals is very important for clarity of mind during the pursuit of those goals.

Understanding the Troubles With Multitasking

Multi-tasking is a subject we have already covered several times. The ability to complete multiple objectives and do several things simultaneously are two different things, and the latter is called multi-tasking.

It has become a norm for people to state that they are multi-taskers while applying for jobs or explaining their abilities.

Multi-tasking can only do one thing for you, and that is to make you look busy. You may create an aura that you are engaged and have too many things on your hands. However, those tasks always remain on your hands and never materialize.

Focus is an ability our mind has developed over millions of years of evolution. Multitasking is only a distraction. It takes away your focus on one thing but never allows you to fix it on another. This way, even your focus goes in suspended animation.

You are working without focus. It leads to indefinite delays and mental clutter. You begin making excuses, and for that, you need to deal with even more clutter.

Multi-tasking will lead to exhaustion, self-esteem issues, and disinterest in the issue.

Paying Attention to Your Routines

If you want to eliminate the clutter in your responsibilities, you need to minus the distractions. Weed out all the things that are wasting your time.

We are slaves of routine. You may feel that you are a spontaneous person, but there are several things that we get used to. Such things can be a big drain on your time.

Are you a coffee person or a tea person?

It is a trick question. Whatever your answer is, you are admitting that you are a slave of habit and routine. First, you get habitual of the beverage and then of the routine to procure it.

Both will waste your time when you begin feeling the need to have it even without real intention to drink it.

If you are already shaking your head in disapproval, replace the beverage desire with your desire to have other things.

Routine is ingrained in us since our childhood, but a blind following of the routine can be dangerous as it keeps you in autopilot and curtails the ability to think mindfully.

For sorting your life and responsibilities, begin paying attention to your routines.

Chapter 13: Decluttering Your Personal Life and Relationships

'Happening' is a word that has added to much clutter to most of us' personal lives. We want our lives to be happening, like others. We have harbored a misconstrued notion that a 'happening' life is a better life. We want to have too much activity and hustle-bustle in life. We want to meet new people and go places.

However, we are never willing to look at the costs involved. Time is precious, also because it is limited. We do not have plenty of it. Even if you live the longest in humanity, it can't be a little more than a hundred years. All of that is not even productive. If you are not managing your time effectively, you are going to be in great trouble.

Most people want to have all the fun in life and also the money to have that fun. In principle, there is nothing wrong with it, but it has time as a limiting factor. You pay the price by exhausting yourself trying to manage both simultaneously.

In the end, the only thing that can exist is mental clutter. You deprive yourself of time, calm, sleep, and money and then spend time worrying about all that.

Wrong notions about personal life are also why people have so much clutter at such an early age. They are unable to strike a balance. Their work-life balance is always in chaos. They are grasping for breath all the time.

Such habits also affect how you conduct your relationships. From mismanagement of time to having too many toxic relationships, the problems can be plenty.

These issues also ultimately add to the mental clutter and make the worse of something that's already bad.

Most people feel that decluttering personal life and responsibilities would require a lot of personal training and management, but it simply needs discipline in reality.

Our emotions are not as big a problem as our habits are beyond our means. We are mismanaging the resources at hand, and that causes all the clutter.

Helpful Steps to Declutter Your Life and Relationships

Learn to Look Beyond Possessions

Materialism has gone deep inside us. Want of things is an eternal desire. We want to have everything that can be had. This mentality is one of the biggest causes of clutter.

Our prime objective in life is to be happy and not to have things. Certain things may add to the comfort that helps us stay happy, but even an excess of those will cause clutter.

Hunting and hoarding have been the prime way of living. Even after thousands of years of moving up the ladder, we cannot get over our hunting and hoarding instincts. Things can only be a means of happiness; they have no power to bring happiness in life. If you are trying to lead a life of a hoarder, peace and happiness may remain evasive.

The desire to have one and then another and then some more will keep your mind cluttered. You will then have the worries of keeping those things. This clutter is perpetual.

Become Thrifty With Time

As we have already discussed, time is a limited commodity. There is no limit to the money you can earn or possessions you can have. However, your time in this world is limited to the final second. It will not move an inch.

Suppose a person is diagnosed with an end-stage critical illness, and the doctors give that person an estimated time of one year. What do you think that person would like to do with that time?

The obvious answer is to finish the most important things first and put things in order.

Sadly, we never realize that all of us come with this limit. That person knows the estimated time left and hence doesn't have the luxury to be very happy.

Fortunately, we come with an expiry date, but that's not written on us, and hence we can live as if we are never going to die. But, that's not entirely true. When you waste time in useless pursuits, you don't realize that it was valuable time that's never going to come back.

The day you develop an understanding of the importance of time, managing mental clutter would become easier.

Create Space in Life

Breathing space is something most people yearn for. Yet, they find no personal space in their life. They are always occupied with something, and soon this leads to exhaustion and lethargy.

A cluttered mind is a very crumpled space. When you have too many things going on simultaneously, it becomes very difficult to have time that you could call your own.

You can never breathe easy as something is always pending and troubling you.

You have too many aspirations, objectives, and desires, and they keep giving you sleepless nights.

Until you declutter your life, its objectives, and responsibilities, you'll never have that space.

It will not happen on its own. You will have to create this space with your conscious efforts.

A clear realization of your objective helps in removing the clutter from the mind. The more balanced your schedule is, the easier you'd feel in your life.

You should also have ample time to be with yourself. Most people underestimate the importance of being with themselves. They begin to lose connection with self and lead lives prescribed by others. The influence of other people and society increases, and the touch with self decreases.

The Myth of Popularity

The desire to be likable and get accepted by society drives many people. They do things only because they want others to recognize them and talk about them. Underconfidence, inferiority complex, intimidation, or disregard in the past also make people aspire for popularity.

There is nothing wrong with aspiring to be popular or being popular. However, that should make your life better and not worse.

Kids these days can go to extreme lengths to be acceptable and popular in their lot. Adults spend more time, money, and energy in trying to impress others and be popular.

When you are trying to be popular, it is important to check whether you are trying to be popular as you or someone else. If you try to be popular as someone else, that can be a huge problem. The real problem with that is comfort.

You will keep pretending to be something that you aren't, and that will only add clutter to your mind. You will always remain on alert in a defensive mode, and this chronic state of alertness can be tiring and frustrating. Pretending to be someone else fills you with insecurities and fears.

Overcoming this mental barrier is very important for clearing out the mental clutter.

Dealing with Toxic Relationships

The Reasons for Toxicity in Relationships

Relationships are at the core of our coexistence. We crave relationships and need them for survival. We can't survive like most animals in the wild do. We do not need companionship only to procreate, as some animals do. Strong emotional attachment is something that forms the basis of human relationships.

However, any relationship in the world can only survive when there is a smooth and proportionate exchange of responsibilities and interdependency.

Striking this balance is the most critical part of relationships.

When we talk of a smooth and proportionate exchange of responsibilities, we are usually subjective. Every individual might have a different perception of rights and responsibilities due and owed.

Love, affection, emotional dependence, and other intangible variables also matter a lot.

Many people can never determine these things properly and get into toxic relationships where one partner becomes parasitic, and they become the host.

It May Only Be Your Perception

When determining whether a relationship is toxic or not, there is a very high likeliness that you might get biased. Responsibilities and exchange of intangible elements are subjective, and your mental clutter can cloud your judgment.

There are times when we begin expecting too much from our partners without even expressing the things we expect. Such expectations are bound to end in disappointments. We can have unrealistic expectations, and that may also add to clutter when not met.

Maintaining a relationship with an individual is not going to be easy. We are dealing with a human being with a functional mind and a different set of expectations.

Reaching a middle ground and discussing the rights and responsibilities is very important. If you do not discuss these things, rifts are bound to form.

Despite these, some relationships may be difficult to handle. Necessarily, they may not be toxic, and a little initiative and clarity of thought can help you make them work.

If you feel that you need to work on your relationships, you can start with:

Inclusiveness

Exclusivity is one of the biggest hurdles in front of stable relationships. Most of us have a very strong sense of identity. It means that we relate to different things differently. It gives birth to our likes, dislikes, preferences, opinions, and other things that become a part of our identity. The more identified we feel with these things, the harder we'll find to accommodate others as they also come with their identifications.

Making relationships work requires a lot of inclusiveness, where you can allow others to be the way they are. Once you do that, dialogue becomes easy, and people easily agree to disagree.

The idea of either convincing or getting convinced can be dangerous in relationships.

Listen

We live in a world where everyone is saying something, but no one is listening. People can hear you, but they are not listening to you. It can be a very frustrating feeling. You feel ignored and humiliated.

We face it every day in some form or the other. However, getting ignored by people, we expect nothing, and getting ignored by someone you love or care for can be different. It instantly gives birth to doubt, insecurities, complaints, dissatisfaction, and discontent.

If you don't want the relationship to turn toxic, you must listen to your partner and stress on your need to be heard. Finding some personal time when you can have a one to one conversation without the distractions like TV, phone, or files is also a great idea.

A simple conversation with your partner and the satisfaction of getting heard can save your relationship from getting toxic. It will also help you prevent clutter in your mind as your thoughts and worries will get an expression.

Speak Mindfully

Mindful speaking is a very important attribute. We can prevent a lot of miscommunication if we speak mindfully.

When people lose their focus on the things they can say and begin saying anything, they cause irreparable damage.

Anything said by you also gives rise to a new train of thoughts even within your mind. Reactionary things can get your mind fixated on those thoughts and cause clutter. When you say something inflammatory, your mind knows that there might be a rebuttal, and it also begins to prepare for a counter-reaction.

If you want to reduce the formation of mental clutter, you must speak mindfully. The more reaction you invoke, the greater would be the damage.

Let Other's Be

We prefer homogeneity. The clutter of color, creed, race, ethnicity, religion, and regionalism results from maintaining homogeneity. However, it isn't possible to have everything the same.

We are all individuals. It means that even if we have everything the same, every person's mind would be different. It would ultimately result in differences in perception, preferences, habits, and ideologies.

If you expect your partner to be as per your desires or trying to fix things in your partner, you will make the relationships toxic.

Relationships are all about enjoying the favorable attributes and compromising with the attributes that may not match your passion.

However, despite your best efforts, relationships can develop stress and fissures.

The main stress points are:

Uncertainty

Some people can never make up their minds about a certain relationship and hence fear commitments, whereas the other partner is constantly demanding. It creates uncertainty. It is not healthy for relationships.

If you want your relationship to work, you must commit and express your desire to your partner openly to know the opinion. Moving it round and round in your mind will only add up more clutter and yield nothing.

Insecurities

We all have certain insecurities, and there is nothing to be ashamed about it. The more we try to hide them, the greater the problems they create. When you try to hide your insecurities in your relationships but expect your partner to act according to them, you breed stress.

Hegemony

We all have a desire to control. No one wants to lose control. However, some people can be very assertive, and they may take away the breathing space from the relationship. They try to make things happen their way, and that is again very troublesome.

The desire to control and dominate the life and feelings of other individuals can cause stress in relationships.

Poor Boundaries

We all need boundaries. It gives us the space to have our identity intact. Some people in the cover of the relationship try to breach these boundaries. They try to intrude in personal space and dominate it. It can never be a welcome act. It will lead to stress in relationships.

You must ensure that you are not a reason for the stress in the relationship. It is the most challenging task to find faults within ourselves because our minds' clutter keeps us pointed towards others.

Any partner can make the relationship toxic. However, you must identify such relationships and get out of them if they are damaged beyond repair.

Some of the symptoms of a toxic relationship are:

Abusiveness

Toxic relationships can get very abusive. There can be physical, mental, emotional, or financial abuse of the partner because the other partner becomes parasitic. The bond of attachment gets severed, and hence there is little empathy and love left.

Lack of Integrity

Toxic relationships have poor integrity because the partner has no or very little mental or emotional attachment. People stay in such relationships only because they want to use the relationship to their advantage. They have already fixed the relationship's expiry date, and they are trying to drain it as much as they can before it reaches the expiry.

Compatibility Issues

Initially, there is a lot of passion involved in relationships. The desires that make us feel attracted to others keep us blinded about the grounds of incompatibility. However, nothing lasts forever, and you realize the number of things you are like is in very much short supply against the things you dislike.

You feel that adjusting with the partner in the long-term might be difficult, and you begin to look for options in place of finding grounds of commonality. At this stage, the relationships are already toxic, and getting out of it at the earliest possible is the best.

The Options You Have

Relationships can get toxic, and you must accept the fact when they do. Trying to push the thought of such a possibility is a mistake many people make for longer than they should. Ignoring the danger doesn't make the danger go away. On the contrary, it keeps you numb with fear and catches you unprepared till the point it strikes you.

Therefore, if you have reached a point where your relationship has become toxic, you must consider:

Life Without That Person

Some people find it very hard to imagine life without a person, and initially, it can become very difficult. However, you can't stretch a relationship for too long if it isn't cohesive anymore.

Living apart is not that difficult as the idea of living apart is. It is natural for us to develop some dependencies and get used to people. However, you will have to accept that you will have to live without that person in the future.

The Agony of Separation

We may have several differences with our partner, but there is also some longing that the subconscious never trows out completely. It can be a cause of agony when you are going through the initial separation phase. Pain and discomfort are usually a part of the package. These things can make people indecisive about a toxic relationship or even make them fickle-minded.

That is a very bad decision to make. Growing apart is always a painful process, but there is no going back once you have stepped in that direction.

Do Not Involve Passion

Bringing a relationship to an end is a difficult decision most of the time. Until you have caught your partner doing something so disastrous that there is no going back, ending relationships is difficult. However, it should never be made ugly.

Even if you are parting ways with your partner, you should ensure that it ends without passions flaring up and leading to something nasty.

You must keep in mind that the more reaction emerges, the stronger will be the impression on your mind, and it will increase the clutter in an already cluttered space.

Handling negative Reaction

Buddhists believe in the concept of 'Karma.' They believe that every action leads to a reaction, and we can't be free of the emotional cobweb until we can release ourselves of this Karma.

Ending relationships is bound to have reactions. However, the more you react, the greater Karma you'll generate and set further escalation in motion. Negativity generally begets more negativity in life. You might feel that you are expressing negative emotions for someone else. You are eventually causing more damage to your mental peace.

You must try to remain calm and not give way to negativity.

Chapter 14: Decluttering Your Home

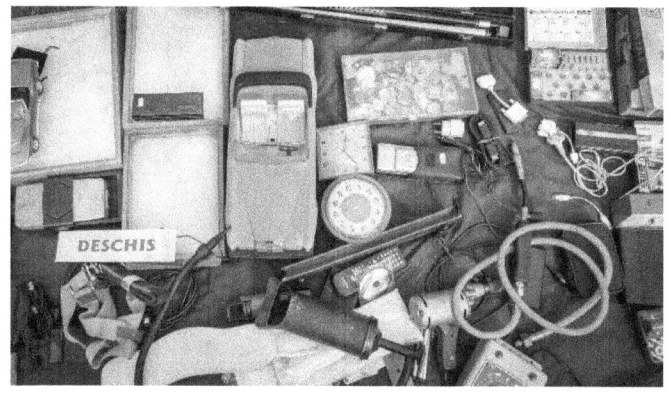

Home is a very important place. It is where you can be yourself without inhibitions. It is a place where you can find peace. However, a cluttered home can do the opposite to you.

Some people believe that if they focus on clearing the mental clutter, the physical clutter will not affect them. It is a misconception.

Decluttering the mind is a comprehensive act. You need to be inclusive and not leave out anything.

Physical clutter around you will always create a distraction and overstimulate your senses. It will never allow you to focus on your priorities.

Make Living Space Livable

You must always ensure that your living space is livable. It must never become a warehouse where you simply collect items.

These are the times of aggressive marketing where people are trying to sell one thing or the other all the time. Even in the dead of the night of you switch on your TV, you'll find advertisements blaring with full enthusiasm.

It is their job to sell things to you, but do you really need those things. It is a very important question that we all need to ask ourselves. Do we really need all the things that we have in our households, and is it really adding value to our lives?

You may be able to recall ten things at the back of mind that you may not have used in a year. Yet, they are present in your home. Are they not adding clutter?

If you want to declutter your home, you must make your living space livable.

The possession of more things not only leads to mental clutter; it also motivates you to possess more. You are on an upward curve.

Until you begin downsizing or removing clutter from your household, you will not be able to think about decluttering in real sense.

Decluttering your home is also a part of the mental decluttering process.

Popular Decluttering Methods

The KonMari Method

It is one of the most objective ways to declutter your home. The best thing about this method is that it helps you adopt a very positive approach towards things and have the lowest resentment levels while disposing of things from your home.

This method focuses on adopting a value-based approach. This approach emphasizes more on keeping important things rather than picking the undesirable. It means you will be investing your energy into identifying the things that add value to your life or the things that are solving or going to solve a purpose shortly.

The method is very simple. You can start with any part of your home. Put all the same category in a pile and then start picking things that are valuable to you. You must pick each item and try to feel if it is precious to you or not. Try to feel if the absence of that thing would matter to you in the long run.

Here, it will be important for you to assess the importance of that thing based on the frequency of use. If it is of any emotional and sentimental value, you must try to remember the last time you revisited it. There are plenty of items in our homes that we keep storing for their emotional value. However, we never revisit those things, or revisiting them brings back painful memories. If something invokes such negative emotions, then it is always in your best interest to let that thing go.

It would help if you also tried to keep things strictly on the prospects of its use. It means if you feel that you will need something in the immediate future, you are more than welcome to keep that thing. However, if you don't know when a thing can be used and have kept it on the 'what if you may need it sometime in the future' basis, then it must go. The chances are that you may never need it. Even if you need it sometime in the distant future, you can always get it. Keeping it in the home to create more clutter is not a very prudent choice.

Every item that you choose to keep must spark joy in you. You should feel happy to keep that thing or must have regular or immediate use.

We are hoarders by nature, and hence, we like to keep duplicates if one breaks down. When things break or get damaged, we don't repair them, they get outdated by the time, and we get new ones. The spares keep rusting and never come to use. So keeping the duplicates is not a very bright idea if you are clearing the clutter.

It is a time-consuming process and can start looking a bit tiresome at times. However, it is a very comprehensive way of decluttering your home as you will be clearing out everything that is not invoking some passion inside you. The remaining things will be valuable and dear to you.

It is a process that helps you place value in your home. You can do this with your relationships, memories, and even your attachments. Only keep the ones that are igniting passion or adding value. Do not cling to your past. Please do not feel obliged to carry the baggage of memories as it makes the journey difficult.

If there are memories that have hurt you, learn from them, and move on. Do not let them haunt you for your whole life. If there are relationships that are getting difficult to manage, get out of them, and move on. Find new ones that make your life happy.

It is a very short and uncertain life. You can move forward with very little. Consider the memories and relationships as the backpack you carry while you go on a trip. Carrying a heavy one is reassuring at times, but it also causes a lot of pain and weighs you down. You always find it difficult to walk with a very heavy backpack, and the journey also becomes less pleasurable.

The lighter you travel, the more comfortable you will be. It will also mean that you will have space to pick new and better things on the way, and you will be light. If you are traveling too heavy, you are devoiding yourself the opportunity to have better things in life.

The KonMari method gives you a very deep insight into the way life should be handled. Most of our worries are not for our future but due to our pasts. We keep the wounds alive and then cry in pain. Washing it off and letting it heal is the best way to lead a happy life.

The 12-12-12 method

It is a very simple decluttering method to execute. This method focuses on taking things at a medium pace and giving yourself time to decide. As the name suggests, it has three parts of equal importance.

You can start from anywhere in your home. You will need to pick items in the group of 12 on a daily or weekly basis.

Things to Put Away

You will have to pick 12 items that you do not regularly use in this category, but you need them. These should be the items that must be of use at least once in a month. If you don't need those things even at this frequency, you should again reconsider putting them under this category. It would help if you found a proper place to store these things under the proper label to retrieve when they are needed.

We generally have hundreds of such things in our homes, but we keep them in such an absent-minded manner that they are never found when needed. Under this method, you must store them under proper labels at a place where they can be easily found. These things should not be treated as junk.

Things to Give Away

These are the things in your home that still have usable life left in them but are not solving any purpose in your homes. For instance, take your clothes. We all have dozens of trousers in our wardrobes. Yet, we regularly wear only a couple of them. 4-5 are the ones that we wear regularly; the rest are only creating want of space in the wardrobe. You don't fit in some of them, or others might have gone out of fashion. Although all those trousers may have usable life left in them, they have lost value for you. You must pick

12 such items at a set frequency and put them for giving away.

Giving away such things will serve a greater purpose. You will always have a positive feeling that those things will serve a positive role for someone who needs them more than you do. You will not feel your money getting wasted without cause, as it is getting put to better use. You will also feel the joy of giving to others in your way.

Things to Throw Away

It is real clutter that keeps on accumulating in the households. We keep storing such items for future use or due to the habit of procrastination. You must pick 12 such items at the set interval for disposing of. It will help you in clearing the clutter from your home.

It is an easy yet very productive routine that allows you to take things at your own pace. You can follow your deadlines and keep clearing the clutter without crumbling under any pressure.

The Minimalist Game

Another decluttering method seems to work magic for many people trying to clear the clutter from their homes. This method's beauty lies in the fact that it initiates you into the decluttering process at a slow speed and then increases the tempo as the days pass.

You never have the feeling like you have been hit by a truck. It picks up the pace as you start making process. You start as slow as picking one item a day and then come to 30 items in a day by the end of the month.

The process is very simple. You start on the 1st of every month. Pick the number of items to remove from your home based on the date of the month. It means that you will be picking 1 item on the 1st and two on the 2nd. On the 15th day, you will be picking 15 items, and on the 30th, you will have to remove 30 items.

You can again restart the process with 1 item on the 1st of the next month. Although this process starts at a very slow pace, you end up removing 496 items from your home in 1 month, and it is huge progress.

This process carries you slowly towards decluttering your home and helps you in building confidence. Picking 30 items in a day may look like a big goal at present, but when you keep doing it regularly, 30 items would feel nothing as the progress is always one more item a day.

However, you will need to remain consistent and do it without missing a day in the month. Soon, you will find that decluttering your home wouldn't remain a very difficult task. It is an easy and interesting process to clear out useless stuff from your home.

The 4-Box Method

It is one easy method for those who feel throwing out things to be a difficult process. It allows them to decide if they want to keep a few things they aren't putting to any good use.

The collector instinct in us stops us from throwing out stuff that we have gathered spending our hard-earned money. We always remain in a dilemma. This method gives you the chance to select a few things and put them in a basket for you to decide later. You can take the cooling-off time and revisit that basket later to see if you have needed the item in the time it was kept in that basket.

The method is similar to the 12-12-12 method. You will be keeping the three basket named put away, give away, and throw away, the only addition being the fourth undecided basket. If you come across whose fate you are not sure about, you can put it in the undecided basket.

It helps you in clearing the clutter at the moment. It means that things will not be sitting in your rooms while you decide about its fate. You will be putting it aside where it wouldn't be put to use. If you need that item within a few days, you can reclaim it. Otherwise, you will have to dispose of it.

Preventing Future Clutter

Be Firm of Your Decision to Prevent Clutter

Embracing minimalism is not a lighthearted decision. It is not one of those resolutions that people make on the new year eves and forget very soon. Embracing minimalism will have an emotional and financial impact on your life. You will be parting away with things that have monetary and emotional value. Most of such actions will be irreversible. Therefore, stepping into it without being resolute can have repercussions.

Lower Your Emotional Attachment to Things

Minimalism will have an emotional impact. You learn to challenge the process of accumulating things. You start asking more questions about the person of people, things, and memories in your life. At times, it can be very emotionally draining. However, emotional jolts are generally very short, and they bring better things in the future. It is a way to discard everything worthless in your life. You should not be afraid and face the odds with courage and determination.

Look at the Things Differently

We learn to give great importance to society and its view. We attach so much importance to society's views that we start functioning like drones run by the society. Minimalism helps you in getting over the norm. It helps you in identifying your needs. It helps you in getting out of the false perception of the rat-race created by society. You would feel less inclined to possess things entirely for impressing others. You will find reasons for possessing things and look for the value those things bring into your life.

Better Relationships

If the modern lifestyle has had the worst impact on something, it is human relationships. It is the age of whirlwind romances and bitter breakups. It all happens because we fail to see the long-term value in relationships and because we don't see the value, we don't give it the just treatment. It is a reason for most of the problems. We form relationships with lightning speed and then start ignoring them even faster. There is no nurturing period.

Minimalism helps you in giving time to an important thing, like a relationship. You have more time and patience at your hand. You have the value system to understand the worth of every relationship. You also have the process of prioritizing things as per needs. All these things lead to healthier and stronger relationships that will last long.

Chapter 15: Decluttering Your Workspace

Decluttering your workspace is not very different from decluttering your home. The principles remain the same. The only difference in the workplace is that you can't throw everything out. There are files to be kept and preserved. There are things to be managed and resources to be shared.

Decluttering your workspace has two parts:

- Decluttering Your Desk
- Dealing with Clutter from Bosses and Coworkers

Dealing with the first is comparatively easier than the second.

Decluttering Your Desk

Decluttering your desk will also require the same process as you might choose to declutter your home. Here, you do not need to throw things out but to index them properly.

Most of the clutter on work desks is due to disorganization. It not only creates clutter but distractions. When you need them, you'll not find them.

To deal with the problem, you must have an indexing system to find documents and files whenever you want.

We are in the internet age where most of the work is one on computers and the internet. Finding files is easy and systematic.

However, that doesn't mean that clutter on your desktop will not bother you or cause distraction. No matter where the clutter is present, it will always be a source of distraction. If your desktop is filled with numerous files and apps, finding the correct one will consume time, and in the meanwhile, some other file or application may gain your attention. The chances of getting distracted are very high when you are working or living in a cluttered space.

The first step in decluttering your workspace is indexing and labeling files and putting them in designated drawers.

If you are decluttering your computer or laptop, you should consider putting files in separate folders and deleting the files you will not need. Most people put files in various folders, and then they have numerous folders on their desktop that they can't even recognize. Decluttering should create another task in front of you.

Your second step should be to declutter your table, workstation, or cubicle. The drawers in our tables tend to become treasure troves. You could find anything in them. A work table doesn't need to be full of surprises.

You must empty all the drawers one by only keep the things that you need. There can be things that you don't need or might need in the distant future; they don't need to be in the immediate reach of your hand where you see them every day. If you must, keep them in a drawer meant for things to be used sparsely.

The things that you need every day must be kept in the top drawers. The level and frequency of use should determine the place of the objects in your drawer.

The third step is to clean the surrounding. You must remove things that are an obstruction in movement or distracting. If you do not need it there, or not solving a specific purpose, it shouldn't be there.

A minimalist approach is very important if you want to keep your workspace organized. It means that you need to designate specific places for articles and place things back from where you took them so that this organization remains intact.

Dealing with Clutter from Bosses and Coworkers

Dealing with people can be a little trickier than things. Especially people in the workplace can be hard to deal with. Most people think that it is a very bad thing.

You must understand that workplace is a competitive environment, and hence you can't expect people to be very cooperative with you. The hardest part is to develop this understanding.

A workplace is like a pack of a lion. The alpha male is always fighting for supremacy. You can't expect people to be nice to you.

Therefore, the first thing you need to do to deal with your bosses and coworkers is to stop expecting. You must not expect anything from them and only do your part.

The second thing that leads to clutter is engagement. People can be chatty, loud, engaging, and irritating. You must understand that people are people; they come in all varieties. You can't control all of them, but if their attitude affects your productivity, you will have to speak up. If you don't speak up, you won't stop thinking about it. The train of thoughts will leave the station and keep moving inside your mind. It will cause more and more clutter. Your mind will not only think about the things said and done by your coworkers but will also keep preparing answers and rebuttals.

It might look like a mentally rewarding exercise; it is very dangerous. It will make you think about something for much longer that has happened in the past.

If you feel that your coworkers are causing distraction or putting undue pressure on you or someone else is trying to take the credit for your work, you should speak.

There is no need to explode or be loud about it, but you must take a stand for yourself.

Most people fail to prevent such intrusions because they fail in setting up boundaries. The let others encroach their personal space and then crib about privacy and distraction.

Speaking up for yourself and setting firm personal boundaries can help you keep the clutter at work out of your life.

Chapter 16: Decluttering Your Time Spent Online

The internet has proven to be one of the biggest changes in recent times. It has revolutionized the way we think, understand, and express ourselves.

In the beginning, the internet was only a medium to exchange information or data. In this age, data has become the new oil. One who controls data also controls the world.

However, in all this, we forget that the data we are talking about is us. We are the data that is getting harnessed, mined, exploited, and used.

For the biggest corporations in the world, your information is the key to success. You are not the consumer anymore, but you have also become a product of many corporations.

Do you think you have a say in all this?

No, you don't have a say. No matter how seriously you campaign about data security and data privacy, the corporations will not stop using your data to sell their products to you.

They will not stop influencing your opinion about things.

Whenever they can, they'll also make you feel and imagine things they want you to think.

Hence, your perspective about the internet and how it is influencing your life should be clear.

This much was for what the damage the internet is causing you without your knowledge and permission.

Earlier, parents used to tell their kids that the outside world is not safe, and hence you must be careful. Now, that insecurity has seeped into our homes in the form of the internet. Today, if not used carefully, the internet is not a safe place for anyone. There are countless ways people will try to influence your opinion and push their agenda in your mind.

Social Media Platforms Cluttering the Mind

There is no doubt that the internet has made it possible to find any kind of information easily. The information that could have taken days to reach the masses reaches like wildfire these days. Revolutions that couldn't have taken place earlier because people didn't have a source to know that they had some support are now taking place like anything. The whole middle east and its Arab Spring is a great example of the power of the internet and social media platforms.

However, there is another aspect of social media too. With the help of social media, shaping public opinion has become comparatively easy. Companies are trying to change your purchasing behavior. Political parties try to change your opinion. Some people try to make money. Some try to use you as a pawn of their ideology.

Social media is a potent weapon, and you are a direct target with unlimited vulnerabilities. It is a fact that makes social media platforms even more dangerous.

We are inherent information hoarders. The pursuit of knowledge has always been our desire. However, we don't have the required filters about the type of information we are picking in. Most people don't even verify the information they are sucking in, and most people can't do that due to the intricate web of lies knitted around the information.

As a result, we keep on absorbing all kinds of information and accumulate clutter in our minds.

We have poor emotional control with a highly impressionable mind. The combination is very bad when it comes to uncontrolled information. We could see what others in our circle are doing, the way they are leading their lives happily, the things they have bought, the places they have visited, and then we want to have all that and do all that.

None of that is really true. Even the people you idolize may be equally jealous of your life or life of someone else, but you don't have a way to know. However, their lies work on your mind and create discontentment, regret, and reaction. Clutter begins like this.

There is no way we can change the way social media is going to be, but you have the power to change the way it influences you.

Declutter Your Feeds

Stay Away From Negative Content: It is human nature to be curious about negative things. We like to see what others are complaining about. We what to know what's creating a rage in others. We might even feel some guilty pleasure when we see people we dislike getting trashed or thrashed on the internet. We especially like celebrities being trolled mercilessly.

Do you know why?

Most of us loath them because we have not been able to reach there. We put ourselves on an ideological pedestal and like to see down upon the celebrities. It is our inner longing to look and feel better, at least in our understanding.

All this negativity is contagious. These petty joys get to your mind and pollute you. There will be an urge to know more, and you'll get more of this negativity.

You must remove all the feeds that are constantly pouring in negativity.

Limit Your Exposure Time

The Internet is getting limitless like your mind. You can never have enough of it. In one minute, more data gets uploaded on Youtube than you can stream in your lifetime. If you do not have limits, you'll keep on adding clutter to your mind. More internet time also means greater mental fatigue. Your active mind gets more and more burdened, processing this information, and your subconscious gets fodder to spring back to you.

Limiting your internet exposure will help you with both.

Declutter Your Posts

Ask the Question 'Why'

We live in a world where fear of missing out is high. People are craving for attention on the internet so much that they don't even differentiate between posting compromising or inflammatory things. Some people are fine with getting popularity even if it comes at the cost of posting their nudes. At the same time, others don't mind inciting a mob simply for the sake of getting noticed.

None of this is good or acceptable. The Internet has given the public a voice, but that doesn't mean that everyone must speak. We have stopped asking why we should post what we are going to post. It leads to reactions then counter-reactions from us. We fail to notice all the while because we are giving way to clutter in our minds. It must stop. You must ask yourself whether posting something is essential, and is it going to offend or hurt others.

Limit Your Posts

A good way to exercise control over your social media posts is limit the number of posts you can do in a day. If you have crossed that threshold for the day, put it off for the next day. The better you exercise this control, the stronger will be your control of social media outrage.

Conclusion

Thank you for making it through to the end of this book. Let's hope it was informative and able to provide you with all of the tools you need to achieve your goals, whatever they may be.

Mental clutter has emerged as a serious problem. It takes away the mental peace and fills life with discomfort and disorder. However, mental clutter usually draws attention when it is already very high. When it has begun making life miserable, people look for ways to address it.

Sadly, there is no shortcut to deal with mental clutter. It is a chronic problem that develops over the years and can take even longer to get addressed.

This book has attempted to explain mental clutter and the ways you can declutter your mind. There are no shortcuts in this book because there are no shortcuts to eliminate mental clutter. There is no way you can trick your mind into thinking anything that it doesn't know.

This book has presented a detailed understanding of mental clutter and its causes. It has also focused on detailing every step that can help you decluttering your mind and finding peace in this chaotic world.

It has been a sincere attempt to explain how to deal with mental clutter effectively. You can get all the benefits of the process by following the simple steps given in the book. I hope that this book is really able to help you in achieving your goals.

Finally, if you found this book useful in any way, a review on Amazon is always appreciated!

www.ingramcontent.com/pod-product-compliance
Lightning Source LLC
Chambersburg PA
CBHW072148100526
44589CB00015B/2141